YOU CAN'T TELL ANYONE

JOANNA RICHARDS

CURRENCY PRESS
The performing arts publisher

CANBERRA YOUTH THEATRE

CURRENT THEATRE SERIES

First published in 2023
by Currency Press
Gadigal Land, PO Box 2287 Strawberry Hills, NSW, 2012, Australia
enquiries@currency.com.au
www.currency.com.au

in association with Canberra Youth Theatre

Typeset by Brighton Gray for Currency Press.
Cover shows, L–R: Blue Hyslop, Jessica Gooding, Thea Jade, Breanna Kelly, Saar Weston.
Cover photography: Adam McGrath.

Currency Press acknowledges the Traditional Owners of the Country on which we live and work. We pay our respects to all Aboriginal and Torres Strait Islander Elders, past and present.

A catalogue record for this book is available from the National Library of Australia

Contents

'To the superficial observer, it will appear as madness'

C.G. Jung

You Can't Tell Anyone was first produced by Canberra Youth Theatre at The Courtyard Studio, Canberra Theatre Centre, Ngunnawal Land, on 10 August 2023 with the following cast:

GWEN	Ella Buckley
TILLY	Emily O'Mahoney
JEREMY	Jake Robinson
WILLA	Jessi Gooding
LUKE	Isaiah Prichard
KAT	Paris Scharkie
BENNY	Lachlan Houen
NICOLE	Breanna Kelly

Director, Caitlin Baker
Set and Costume Designer, Kathleen Kershaw
Lighting Designer, Ethan Hamill
Sound Designer and Composer, Patrick Haesler
Stage Manager, Rhiley Winnett

Writer's Note

After Nietzsche declared that 'God is Dead' it was Carl Jung's hope that God could be revived in our own subconscious. He was distressed by the shortcomings of rationality to explain the workings of the world and our minds. This loss of religion is something that I think can be applied to young adults who are quickly learning that their parents aren't gods, their prayers won't be answered, and that there is no perfect explanation for everything that happens. The chaotic search for a meaningful order to replace religion (whatever its form) is inevitable.

The subconscious adherence to a strong collective consciousness is something that I think is particularly relevant to youth today. The world is in a period of great uncertainty. Every day is tinged by the threat of natural disaster, disease and war. Fact has given way to opinion. Dogged belief has outrun rationalism. Chaos looms just outside everyone's adherence to their own niche flimsy collective conscious. What once seemed like madness now seems sensible as we struggle to retain any sense of meaning, order and belonging.

Why do we do nonsensical things? Even when they disadvantage us? Why do we stay at a party when we are having a terrible time? Why do we continue to associate with people who have hurt us deeply? These questions are more relevant today than ever. A culture of normlessness has produced a generational anomie; a melancholy caused by an inability to see where or how one fits into the world. It's melodramatic and surreal, and that's exactly what it feels like to be a teenager in the world today.

We often underestimate the depth and complexity of teenagers' minds because of the way they speak about topics. However, the issues that play on the minds of young adults are the same ones that have haunted philosophers for years. In this play, although never stated explicitly, the ensemble grapples with philosophical problems such as: Plato's Cave, Aristotle's Good Life, Kant's Conception of Autonomy, Schopenhauer's Unconscious Repression, Nietzsche's Gay Science, Wittgenstein's Weltbild, Heidegger's Being, Arendt's Origins of

Totalitarianism, Sartre's Existentialism, De Beauvoir's Objet De Faire, Freud's Hysteria, Jung's Paranoia, Derrida's Hauntology, Foucault's Discursive Sexualities, Baudrillard's Simulacra, Durkheim's Anomie, Debord's Spectacle, Lasch's Narcissism, and Fisher's Capitalist Realism. The questions of philosophy, which are also often central to art, are at their base *human* questions. Ideas that make up the fabric of our world before we even fully comprehend them.

Joanna Richards
July 2023

CHARACTERS

GWEN, 18, type A perfectionist, aspirational

TILLY, 16, shy and non-conformist, outcast

JEREMY, 18, rational and dependable, caretaker

WILLA, 17, sexy and innocent, bombshell

LUKE, 18, confident and brash, golden boy

KAT, 17, cynical and sardonic, contrarian

BENNY, 18, loud and proud, sidekick

NICOLE, 18, cautious and reserved, watchman

SETTING

The action takes place in the loungeroom and kitchen of a suburban home. A single door into the kitchen should be the initial point of entry for all characters except Tilly and Jeremy. Stairs go off the loungeroom, as does a door to a bathroom.

NOTES

A forward slash (/) in the text indicates the point which the next speaker interrupts.

Conversations often overlap and occur concurrently. As a rule, speech should continue to be directed to the character with whom the dialogue originated.

This play text went to press before the end of rehearsals and may differ from the play as performed.

Lights up on a family room. It is both strange and familiar. Worn but outgrown. TILLY *sits alone on the stage. She is happy.* JEREMY *bursts through the door.*

JEREMY: I knew I had it somewhere.

TILLY: What is it?

JEREMY: Just a little something I want you to have. Here.

　　　He puts a necklace on her.

TILLY: It's pretty.

JEREMY: It's not expensive or anything. I got it for my mum when I was like seven.

TILLY: Are you sure you want me to have it?

JEREMY: Yeah definitely.

TILLY: [*giggling*] Wow.

JEREMY: I remember wanting to make her smile so bad. It was right after Dad left. And I begged my auntie to help me get her a present. And when I gave it to her, she smiled so big.

TILLY: It worked.

JEREMY: Yeah, and she always said I gave her her smile back.

TILLY: That's sweet.

JEREMY: So, I'm hoping maybe I can give yours back to you.

　　　Pause.

　It's corny, ah. It's too corny for you.

TILLY: It is corny. But I like it.

　　　TILLY *and* JEREMY *stare at each other as if they are about to kiss.*

JEREMY: It looks so damn pretty on you. Hang on, let me get my phone so I can take a picture.

　　　JEREMY *runs upstairs.* TILLY *lies down on the floor. She giggles and squirms. She sits up.* GWEN *walks through the door.*

GWEN: You look happy.

TILLY: What? No, I don't.

GWEN: You were smiling.

TILLY: No.

GWEN: It's not a bad thing, it's nice.

TILLY: Don't be weird.

GWEN: I'm not.

TILLY: Why are you here?

GWEN: I live here.

TILLY: But you were meant to be out.

GWEN: Yeah, and I was and then Jeremy ditched me, so I had to catch an Uber, but some people are coming over here now.

TILLY: What? Now?

GWEN: Yes now.

TILLY: But—

GWEN: Tilly, please don't, you can literally just go to your room and chill.

JEREMY *runs down the stairs and is shocked to see* GWEN.

JEREMY: Gwen.

GWEN: Jer, what are you doing here?

Pause.

You left me at the party, and you were supposed to be my ride home—

JEREMY: Shit.

GWEN: —pretty bad boyfriend behaviour—

JEREMY: I'm sorry.

GWEN: —to leave your girlfriend stranded—

JEREMY: No, I—

GWEN: —actually super-embarrassing.

JEREMY: I went to check on my mum.

GWEN: Oh.

JEREMY: Yeah.

GWEN: No, of course.

JEREMY: I just had a bad feeling in my gut that I couldn't shake.

GWEN: No bubba, don't even. Of course, I understand. Come here.

GWEN *cuddles* JEREMY *and kisses his cheeks.*

JEREMY: She's fine.

GWEN: She has a nurse with her tonight, right?

JEREMY: Yeah. But I just wasn't really in the mood for a party, so I thought I'd meet you back here.

GWEN: Shit.

JEREMY: What?

TILLY: Gwen invited everyone back here.

GWEN: I'm sorry babe, not everyone just a few people.

JEREMY: Who?

GWEN: Just like …

TILLY: Did you ask Mum?

GWEN: Mum isn't here.

TILLY: Yeah, but it's still her house.

GWEN: Mum left me in charge.

TILLY: That doesn't answer my question.

GWEN: When she gets back tomorrow, she won't even be able to tell that anyone was here.

TILLY: So, no.

GWEN: Why are you being so annoying?

TILLY: Why are you bringing people over here?

GWEN: Because there is nothing wrong with here.

Pause.

TILLY: I don't want them here.

GWEN: Well, too bad Tilly.

JEREMY: Gwen.

GWEN: What? She can't just stomp her feet and get what she wants all the time.

JEREMY: Yeah but—

GWEN: I want to have one party. It has been a shitty, shitty year and I want to have one party.

JEREMY: Baby there'll be other parties!

GWEN: No! Willa leaves in like a week, we leave in a week, and Benny and Kat go the week after that.

JEREMY: People will always come back home.

GWEN: They might not babe, school's done for us.

JEREMY: It's not like tonight is the last time we'll ever see each other.

GWEN: School is literally the only thing holding us together.

TILLY: Some friends.

GWEN: Okay Tilly, I get it, thank you.

TILLY: They barely talk to you anymore.

GWEN: You know what, I understand that. I don't know if I'd know what to say in their situation. It's been a tough year for everyone.

TILLY: No. It's been a tough year for us. Nothing happened to them.

GWEN: Listen. I—I'm the one who throws the parties. That's what I do, and I want to throw a party just one more time. And I'm seriously so pissed that you are being like this.

TILLY: I don't want people here.

GWEN: Dad would have wanted me to do this.

TILLY: You don't know what Dad would want, don't do that.

GWEN: Tilly, I know you've built this whole new personality around being a victim, but it's the end of school for me. That's a big deal. And I am choosing to be happy. Please choose to do the same.

TILLY: No.

GWEN: Then go upstairs.

TILLY: No.

GWEN: Listen. I love you. You are free to hang out with my friends. But I'm having this party. And I'm having fun tonight.

The group enters through the side door.

WILLA: Well, I wasn't just going to leave it there.

BENNY: You're psychotic.

WILLA: No, I was being humane.

BENNY: You reversed over it.

LUKE: It was full fucking looking at us.

WILLA: I put it out of its misery.

LUKE: It was like daring you to run it the fuck over.

WILLA: I didn't do it on purpose!

KAT: Willa hit a possum and then she made us all get out of the car and pray over its body.

BENNY: Yeah, we went full-on cult.

GWEN: What?!?

LUKE: That's why we're late.

WILLA: I tried to stop, Gwen.

KAT: She did.

WILLA: But it like ran under my car.

TILLY: Wait, you prayed.

BENNY: We would have looked so weird.

WILLA: I felt bad.

TILLY: Are you religious?

WILLA: No, but I needed to do something.

KAT: Technically I don't think animals go to heaven.

GWEN: Really?

WILLA: Kat, you're not religious either.

KAT: Yes, I am, like aesthetically.

LUKE: What does that mean?

KAT: I'm into like the art and the culture and the ideas, you know the vibes.

BENNY: Religion is very trendy right now, actually.

KAT: I think you did the right thing, Wills.

WILLA: Thank you.

KAT: It's nice to honour things.

WILLA: Right?

KAT: Don't project your negative bullshit on to her, guys.

WILLA: Yeah!

> LUKE *goes over to* JEREMY. KAT *and* BENNY *take in the room.*

LUKE: Mate, where'd you piss off to?

BENNY: Is this the room? Where he, y'know …

KAT: Stop.

JEREMY: I had to check on something.

LUKE: Righto, hope you had a good time checking.

BENNY: I'm just asking 'cause it's like spooky / if it …

TILLY: It's not haunted.

GWEN: [*to* LUKE] He went to check on his mum. He was worried. So just be gentle tonight, okay?

LUKE: Oh shit, okay thanks for the heads-up.

KAT: Don't listen to him Tilly, he's an idiot.

> *Multiple conversations overlap.*

WILLA: Gwen, you're living on campus, right?

GWEN: No Jez and I are getting an apartment.

BENNY: I'm so glad I'm taking the year off.

WILLA: Like you'll be living together.

GWEN: Yeah.

TILLY: Aren't you worried you won't go back, Benny?

WILLA: Like just the two of you?

GWEN: Yes.

BENNY: No. I'll be fine. Strong mind.

WILLA: Crazy.

GWEN: Why?

WILLA: I don't know, it just feels like a lot of pressure.

BENNY: Year 12 is exhausting, Till, you wouldn't understand.

GWEN: How is that pressure?

WILLA: The love bit is great. Like I'd love someone to like love me enough to want to like live with me and shit.

TILLY: It's just school.

WILLA: But it's also like oh my God. You live with me? You know?

BENNY: No, it's the drama of Year 12. I can't explain it.

GWEN: I guess. I mean, I don't feel that way and like neither does Jeremy.

WILLA: Have you decided what you'll do?

KAT: Stop being a victim, Benny, admit you want to party for a year.

GWEN: I'm doing arts law.

WILLA: I didn't know you wanted to be a lawyer!

TILLY: What are you going to do, Kat?

GWEN: No, I don't I just got the ATAR for it. And Jeremy likes it in Melbourne. So, Melbourne is good for both of us.

KAT: I want to do clinical psych.

WILLA: Right.

GWEN: Figured a law degree never hurt anyone.

LUKE: You know you get extra points on your ATAR if you are pregnant?

TILLY: That's like two degrees, psych, isn't it?

KAT: Yeah.

JEREMY: That's sexist, what if you like fathered a child?

LUKE: Nope, got to be pregnant.

TILLY: That's going to cost a lot of money.

GWEN: What my degree? Don't / worry about it.

TILLY: No I was talking to Kat.

GWEN: Maybe we should play a game or something?

KAT: Oh, I'm just going to put it on HECS.

LUKE: If someone in our year had died, that would have got us extra points too.

LUKE *sits down next to* TILLY.

Hey Tilly, you're looking good.

GWEN: Absolutely not. Not going to happen.

LUKE: What?? I'm just being friendly.

GWEN: Get up. She doesn't need friends.

BENNY: I wish you could get a HECS loan for being alive.

TILLY: Sorry Luke.

WILLA: That's called a credit card.

JEREMY: People are so selfish.

BENNY: Yeah, but you have to pay a credit card back.

WILLA: Yeah, you have to pay HECS back.

BENNY: No, you don't.

GWEN: One hundred percent you do.

BENNY: Oh, then what's the point?

TILLY: Clinical psych will be a lot of HECS though.

KAT: Yeah, I thought about doing it through the army. But then I'm like low-key concerned they could send me to war.

LUKE: What war?

KAT: The one with Russia, I guess.

LUKE: Oh true.

JEREMY: Or the China one.

LUKE: What China one?

JEREMY: The one that's gonna happen.

LUKE: You really think so?

JEREMY: Probably.

GWEN: Why do boys know so much about war?

LUKE: 'Cause war is fucking sick.

GWEN: No but I mean you could use that space in your brain for useful information like, I don't know, CPR or something.

JEREMY: They wouldn't send a psychologist to the frontline.

KAT: Actually, Jeremy, the real battleground is the mind. I don't want to even think about the fucked up shit the army might make me do.

LUKE: Oh, shit yeah, psyops.

LUKE *sits down on the couch next to* KAT.

Kat what are your labels these days?

KAT: I don't do labels.

LUKE: Ooo edgy.

KAT: You give yourself some hyper-specific label and then complain about how no-one ever treats you as an individual—

GWEN: Willa, drink?

KAT: —and all anyone ever talks about are labels.

WILLA: Yes please.

KAT: I'm not a product, if people want to get to know me, they can just ask.

LUKE: I honestly just want to know who you sleep with.

KAT: Luke, I am literally attracted to everyone except you.

LUKE: Why does that make you more attractive to me?

WILLA: Because you are disgusting.

JEREMY: Luke, drink?

BENNY: I hate labels too.

LUKE: What's on offer?

WILLA: Benny, you don't need a label.

KAT: Ha! Truuue.

BENNY: I actually wasn't being funny.

JEREMY: A little bit of everything?

WILLA: Awwww. Come and make a memory with me.

> WILLA *pulls out her phone and begins to take selfies.*

LUKE: Then I guess I'll have a little bit of everything!

BENNY: [*to* WILLA] Wait, you're going to UTS?

WILLA: USyd.

BENNY: I look foul, delete that one.

WILLA: No. Wait I'm going to shake the phone, so it looks like the photo was taken by accident.

BENNY: What are you actually studying?

WILLA: Engineering.

LUKE: She's joking, she's gonna be one of those hot nurses.

JEREMY: Nurse practioner, actually.

WILLA: No, I'm serious, I want to build bridges.

GWEN: Luke what are you doing?

LUKE: Sports science.

TILLY: What is that?

LUKE: I don't really know what it entails but like it's my passion, y'know?

KAT: You're amazing.

LUKE: Actually, Wills, you should be a physio 'cause then you'd get to feel / up all the footy players.

WILLA: You are actually so repulsive.

KAT: He's like a creature in a zoo to me, I just want to observe.

LUKE: Make a little WAG out of yourself.

BENNY: One step back in the evolutionary chain, he is.

WILLA: How does your brain think of these things?

BENNY: Willa, you'd actually make a great WAG.

KAT: No, she's going to be a woman in stem, stop gatekeeping.

JEREMY: Luke. Focus.

LUKE: Let's just make a fucking monster drink, hey.

WILLA: Thank you, Kat.

LUKE: Hey Benny, that medication you are on?

KAT: You are literally going to make shit just float in the sky, like that's what a bridge does.

BENNY: My epilepsy drugs?

LUKE: Yeah, do they like *do* anything?

BENNY: Like stop me having seizures.

LUKE: Yeah, but I mean like anything else.

WILLA: Yeah, I'm going to make shit float!

KAT: That's crazy. That's so fucking cool!

BENNY: Um no. Sorry.

LUKE: Nah nah nah you're cool. Just wondering.

WILLA: Oh my God do you remember when we …

    WILLA *looks at* GWEN, *stopping herself.*

GWEN: What?

WILLA: No, it doesn't matter.

GWEN: Say it.

WILLA: It's just a memory.

GWEN: About here? And …

WILLA: Yeah.

GWEN: Oh.

WILLA: Do you mind if we—?

GWEN: No, I want you to.

WILLA: Okay I didn't want to make it / weird or sad or anything.

GWEN: I'd rather hear nice things about him, you know—

WILLA: Of course.

GWEN: —than all of us just avoiding it.

 Pause.

LUKE: It's so crazy being in this room, hey?

WILLA: I know, I was just thinking about when we were little.

BENNY: [aside to KAT] It's weird. This is the room where he—

KAT: Shh.

WILLA: Like I feel like so many of my core memories happened in this room.

BENNY: Kat got drunk for the first time in this room—

GWEN: On Pimms, so weird.

BENNY: —and threw up on that couch and we had to lie to your mum about why we needed laundry detergent.

KAT: Thanks for reminding everyone.

BENNY: That's what friends are for.

GWEN: What did we even say?

WILLA: We said we had learnt about chemicals in detergent that are bad for the environment and we wanted to do an experiment.

LUKE: That was a good fucking lie.

TILLY: There is no way Mum believed that.

BENNY: No, she did.

GWEN: She probably just went along with it.

WILLA: Benny was like gagging as he scrubbed, I can see it so clearly.

BENNY: I was the only one who would touch it, who else is out here doing that for you?

LUKE: Remember how your dad would do little psychological experiments / on us …

TILLY: They weren't experiments.

LUKE: Make us play games, whatever, same thing.

GWEN: No but you make it sound like we were part of the Stanford Prison Experiment / or something—

JEREMY: No he—we had fun!

GWEN: —when we were just playing kids' games.

WILLA: Yeah, but he did use them in his books.

JEREMY: I loved it.

LUKE: Yeah, me too.

KAT: I liked the Mafia one.

BENNY: Oh, and what was the secret one?

LUKE: I feel like we should have got credit in the studies.

WILLA: What was the one where we had the blindfolds on? And it was like hide and seek. I think I got a concussion that day.

GWEN: What do you mean?

LUKE: Like are we even mentioned anywhere in any of his books?

KAT: Is the blindfold one the one that made Till cry?

GWEN: I mean I don't think so?

TILLY: I was scared. I'm younger than you guys, come on.

LUKE: All those hours for what?

WILLA: We were just playing games.

LUKE: Yeah, but he was observing us and then writing about it.

TILLY: For the advancement of psychology.

GWEN: We should play a game tonight. Not like a kids' game. But a drinking game or something.

BENNY: I don't care about psychology, I just wanna be famous. We deserve credit.

> WILLA *takes a photo of herself and starts taping on her phone.* KAT *looks at the bookshelf.*

GWEN: Ooo, where's that going?

WILLA: Nowhere.

BENNY: Eugh. See, that's what I need.

GWEN: What?

BENNY: If I looked like her, I'd have a million followers.

TILLY: There's actually more to it than that.

BENNY: I know that. I actually know exactly how much work it takes. It's criminal that I wasn't born into a thot dynasty like the Hadids. I was made for it.

> GWEN *spots* KAT *holding a red book.*

GWEN: Put that back.

KAT: Sorry I didn't—

GWEN: No sorry I shouldn't have … It's my dad's.

KAT: Oh, shit.

TILLY: His last one. He didn't publish it.

KAT: What's it about?

GWEN: Paranoia.

LUKE: I get so paranoid when I'm high.

TILLY: He basically says paranoia happens when your imagination starts to blur with the truth.

WILLA: I have like a crazy active imagination.

BENNY: Oh my God, same.

GWEN: It's basically where your beliefs become so strong that you manifest them or something.

KAT: That's awesome.

TILLY: It's got some really cool ideas.

LUKE: Oh, my fucking God, we should play Paranoia.

JEREMY: What's that?

WILLA: Like you should see my dreams.

BENNY: I had a dream like last night that some farmer was chasing me, but I had the cure for MS.

KAT: Is your mum going to publish it?

BENNY: But then like I just had to get to Egypt?

GWEN: I don't know, it gets a bit weird.

LUKE: Wait you don't know what paranoia is, Jer?

JEREMY: I know what paranoia is.

KAT: Weird how?

LUKE: The game though, have you never played before?

JEREMY: Nah.

WILLA: I dreamt I bought our school—

GWEN: [to KAT] I don't know it's just …

WILLA: —and I made it like my house and had like twenty kids—

GWEN: It's different to his other stuff.

LUKE: Okay, we *have* to play then. Guys, we are playing Paranoia.

WILLA: —but I was also like an undercover sleeper agent.

TILLY: The book's unhinged, it doesn't make any sense.

BENNY: My stepmum is actually like a medium, I bet she could tell you what that means.

WILLA: Yeah, 'cause it was like a lot.

KAT: Can I look at it?

GWEN: I—

    KAT *grabs the book off the shelf.*

LUKE: Gwen, we are going to play Paranoia.

GWEN: What?

LUKE: You said you wanted to play a game; we came up with a game.

BENNY: 'Cause, you know, like I don't really see you having that many kids.

WILLA: No neither.

LUKE: We are going to play Paranoia, 'cause of your dad's book thing. In his honour.

BENNY: You could totally be a spy though!

GWEN: I don't—I've never played.

KAT: YES.

WILLA: Maybe *I* should go into the army?

BENNY: True.

KAT: We have to play. It's so fun.

TILLY: Can I play?

KAT: And it lines up! It's like meant to be.

TILLY: Gwen?

GWEN: Yeah okay, fuck it, let's play.

WILLA: I was thinking …

LUKE: Willa, shut up we are playing Paranoia.

WILLA: Ooo, fun!

BENNY: Oh shit, I haven't played that in so long.

JEREMY: Paranoia sounds like a risky game though, guys.

WILLA: It is but that's what makes it fun.

LUKE: Yesssss this is such a good idea. Why do I have all these great ideas?!

KAT: Everyone be quiet, I'm going to go through the rules.

WILLA: Okay.

LUKE: [*chanting*] Play. The. Game. Play. The. Game.

GWEN: Shhh!

KAT: We are playing Paranoia.

LUKE: [*to* TILLY] Sit here.

    GWEN *shakes her head;* TILLY *sits next to* JEREMY.

TILLY: [*to* JEREMY] Boo!

KAT: You play by whispering a question into your neighbour's ear like so …

Whispers in WILLA*'s ear.*

And then my neighbour will answer the question out loud. Go.

WILLA: Oh. Um. Tilly.

KAT: And then we flip like a coin.

GWEN: We don't have a coin.

KAT: I'll just pretend for now.

LUKE: You ask the question; you flip the coin …

KAT: If it's heads, you say the question out loud. Tails, it remains a secret.

TILLY: So, if it's tails there is no way to find out?

KAT: Nope. Take it to the grave.

She flips an imaginary coin.

Oh my God! It's heads. Willa, tell Tilly the question.

WILLA: Who's the most likely to fall asleep in public.

TILLY: Um, okay?

LUKE: What a boring question.

WILLA: Did I offend you?

KAT: It's just for the explanation. No-one is offended.

LUKE: I don't want to play with boring questions like that.

BENNY: I already have a fucked-up question in my head.

GWEN: Does anyone have a coin?

KAT: Because it can get pretty heated, I think we have to play until everyone has had their name dropped at least once, to keep it fair.

BENNY: No boring questions.

KAT: Yeah, okay we will play on high heat.

BENNY: Obviously.

GWEN: We will keep it fun, though.

KAT: Fuck it, it's like the last time we'll all be together anyway.

LUKE: Okay, I'm so down for this.

JEREMY: So, we play until?

TILLY: Whenever we want to stop.

KAT: No. Until there's no more secrets.

BENNY: Why'd you say that all sinister.

KAT: Upping the stakes.

WILLA: Oh my God! I'm nervous.

GWEN: Or we can just play until we want to stop.

TILLY: There is no stopping.

KAT: Ooooo spooky.

TILLY: No, I'm bought in. Evil vibes all the way.

KAT: Gwen said that the book is about being paranoid. And that paranoia is caused by the shit you don't know so …

JEREMY: I don't know …

LUKE: I want to play the game!

> LUKE *starts grunting in a rugby game fashion.*

BENNY: No paranoia if you know everything.

GWEN: Radical honesty.

KAT: Oh, shit that's the other thing. You have to have to have to tell the truth. Otherwise, it's no fun.

BENNY: But theoretically.

KAT: Theoretically what?

BENNY: Like how would you know if I lied?

WILLA: You can't lie.

BENNY: I'm just saying what if I did?

TILLY: Why would you lie?

GWEN: I'm going to go get a coin.

> GWEN *leaves to find a coin.*

LUKE: I'm just saying, if we all got naked—

BENNY: How would that keep people honest?

LUKE: Not saying it would, just throwing out options.

TILLY: We tell the truth for my dad.

> *Silence.*

KAT: [*supporting* TILLY] Yeah, for Pops. For science. Tilly is right, we play the game properly because, we always played the games properly.

WILLA: I'm down for that.

LUKE: Get that book.

JEREMY: Why?

LUKE: I'm going to write my name in it.

BENNY: What?

WILLA: You can't do that.

LUKE: Why not?

JEREMY: It's not yours.

LUKE: We all should. We were a part of it. We deserve a credit.

KAT: No, it's disrespectful.

LUKE: We are going to play a game of Paranoia; this is a book about paranoia. It makes sense. It will keep us honest.

JEREMY: Luke.

LUKE: It's like honouring something we did here.

WILLA: You mean like as a way of remembering, like our childhood?

LUKE: Yeah!

JEREMY: I think that's a bad idea.

LUKE: Why?

JEREMY: At least wait for Gwen.

LUKE: Why?

BENNY: I am of the opinion that you don't mess with things like that. Especially given, y'know …

KAT: The circumstances.

LUKE: We were involved in like *all* of this.

KAT: It's like desecration or something, isn't it?

LUKE: It's a book.

WILLA: Yeah, I agree.

LUKE: That's bullshit.

BENNY: No, it's not, there are like consequences for things.

KAT: Yeah, you don't touch dead people's stuff.

> LUKE *writes his name on the front page of the book.*

TILLY: Oh my God.

LUKE: There, it's done.

JEREMY: Til, you okay?

> GWEN *re-enters.*

WILLA: Gwen.

GWEN: What are you doing?

LUKE: We are writing our names in the book.

GWEN: Nobody said you could do that.

JEREMY: It's to honour your dad.

GWEN: Nobody said you could do that.

KAT: It's so we play the game for him.

JEREMY: It's like a commitment.

BENNY: To play the game properly.

LUKE: Yeah, to tell the truth.

GWEN: Nobody said you could do that.

TILLY: I'll do it.

GWEN: What?

LUKE: Okay, here we go!

TILLY: I wanna play. For Dad.

BENNY: Yeah, for your dad.

GWEN: Why are you being like this?

TILLY: Like what?

> TILLY *pushes past* GWEN *to go and get a drink.* LUKE *is pushing the book in* WILLA*'s face.*

WILLA: I don't want to—

LUKE: Just do it!

WILLA: No, it feels wrong.

LUKE: Why?

WILLA: It feels dangerous or something.

JEREMY: What like ghosts and spirits and shit?

WILLA: Yeah, maybe.

KAT: Wait, did Benny tell you about his stepmum? She speaks to dead people or something.

BENNY: I'll sign it. I'm not fussed.

WILLA: No, Benny.

LUKE: How do you believe this shit? Like actually this is why people hate women.

KAT: Whoa.

JEREMY: Dude, no.

LUKE: You're laughing 'cause you know I'm right.

GWEN: No, he's laughing because he can't believe you would actually say that out loud.

TILLY: Jeremy, sign the book.

GWEN: What the fuck, Tilly. Jeremy, no.

TILLY: Do it.

JEREMY: Luke and Tilly already did it, so I don't see what the big deal is.

LUKE: It's true! All that astro-crystal crap, it's like you go out of your way to make yourself believe nonsense.

WILLA: I bet every woman in this room is smarter than you.

GWEN: Jeremy! I—what—why did you do that?

TILLY: [*to* LUKE] You believe in science?

LUKE: Yeah, what's your point.

TILLY: How is that different?

LUKE: Um are you kidding?

TILLY: No, I'm not kidding how is your belief different from my belief?

JEREMY: It's not a big deal.

GWEN: It's a big deal to me, I asked you not to do it.

BENNY: Pass it here.

KAT: Wait, Til, do you actually, like actually, believe believe in this stuff? Like the same way you do medicine and gravity?

LUKE: If you need to me to explain how the scientific method is different from believing a book is going to be mad at me, then I'm actually at a loss.

TILLY: Sounds like you can't explain.

GWEN: Jeremy.

JEREMY: What? Please just grab a drink and have some fun, isn't that what you wanted?

TILLY: How much science do you actually know?

LUKE: Um, I know all the science.

GWEN: Fine.

She goes to pour herself a drink. KAT *joins her.*

TILLY: I have a feeling you wouldn't know your way out of a paper bag when it comes to science.

LUKE: Look all I am saying is I haven't seen any evidence for spirits or crystals or any of that.

BENNY: Wait, so are we doing the name thing or … ?

TILLY: But you have for Quantum Mechanics?

WILLA: Quantum Mechanics are sick.

BENNY: Yes? No?

LUKE: As if you know about Quantum Mechanics.

WILLA: I'm going to be an engineer! You know this!

LUKE: How can you want to be an engineer and believe in ghosts?

JEREMY: [*to* BENNY] Yes. Do it. Tilly did it.

WILLA: I'm not saying I believe in it, I am just saying it's better to be careful with these things.

TILLY: You are being like weirdly dogmatic about science. Any actual scientist will tell you that they don't know things for sure. It's like, correlations that seem right.

LUKE: And this, what, 'correlation' seems like right to you?

TILLY: I guess.

LUKE: You sound like a conspiracy theorist.

WILLA: That's kinda how science starts, mate.

LUKE: Okay, you've lost me.

> KAT *takes the book off* BENNY.

KAT: I'm writing my name since we've already messed with it.

LUKE: Willa, how is science a conspiracy theory?

BENNY: [*to* JEREMY] Are you more scared of like ghosts or serial killers?

JEREMY: Serial killers for sure.

WILLA: All of science is built on like theory.

BENNY: Why?

JEREMY: Um, because they are real.

LUKE: And the conspiracy part?

WILLA: I don't know like the scientific community working as a team? Peer review?

BENNY: Yeah, but that means you can like really kill them, right?

JEREMY: Right.

BENNY: But how do you kill a ghost?

JEREMY: Who hasn't signed the book yet?

KAT: Would you have sex with a ghost?

WILLA: Ew.

GWEN: [*to* JEREMY] I mean I haven't.

BENNY: Whose ghost?

WILLA: Oh my God, would you!?

JEREMY: [*to* GWEN] Do you want to?

KAT: Um … Wait who is your dead 'would'?

BENNY: Oh, good question!

> *Pause.*

Malcolm X.

KAT: Interesting!

GWEN: I don't know.

LUKE: Just do it.

BENNY: He's hot for starters, but also people say he was like bi or gay but what's the proof, you know? So I just want to check it's not like stolen valour. 'Cause like he already has a lot of valour.

WILLA: Wait Gwen, you don't have to.

LUKE: This is the next generation of engineer, everyone. Freaked out about a book and thinks science is a conspiracy theory.

TILLY: Most conspiracy theories are anti-Semitic right?

KAT: Wait, what?

WILLA: Alright genius. You win. There's no theory in science. We just know everything already.

TILLY: I don't know, I read that like if you follow almost any conspiracy back to its roots it's probably about hating Jewish people.

BENNY: What about Princess Diana?

TILLY: What about Princess Diana?

GWEN: Oh my God, I love Princess Diana.

BENNY: How is that about hating Jewish people?

LUKE: Willa where's the science in the theory that the Queen killed Princess Diana?

WILLA: I don't think anyone is saying the Queen killed Diana.

TILLY: Gwen thinks she is Diana Spencer.

GWEN: No that makes me sound crazy. I just—I don't know. I really relate to her, I guess.

KAT: Both self-centred bulimics so that tracks.

WILLA: Kat!

GWEN: I actually don't do that anymore so fuck you.

KAT: [*through teeth*] Yeah now she just doesn't eat.

BENNY: I actually think Diana is kind of basic.

GWEN: No! She was the people's princess. She was like perfect.

BENNY: But! I love that she was such a victim.

GWEN: What are you talking about?

BENNY: Like she was always boo hooing about how the media was chasing her.

GWEN: They were, they killed her—

LUKE: [*muted trumpet*] Bow bow.

BENNY: Yeah, but she just *loved* to talk about it. Like 'wah I'm depressed, I cut myself'. Women love love love to talk about their Ls, you know? I'm for it personally.

GWEN: Why are you all being so misogynistic tonight? Oh my God.

BENNY: It's not misogynistic, it's just the truth. Also, I'm gay.

GWEN: So?

KAT: She did have like huge lie-down-on-the-floor energy.

BENNY: So true.

TILLY: What are you two talking about?

BENNY: Oo! You would get this, Tilly. You know how the earth is actually like a huge battery? Well, women like instinctually know to get close to it when they are overwhelmed. That's why they faint and collapse.

GWEN: That's sexist! What are you guys doing?

BENNY: No, that's science.

KAT: Yeah, and he's gay.

BENNY: Exactly.

JEREMY: Gwen, write your name.

GWEN: I don't even understand why we are doing it.

KAT: To honour what we did here. In this room. And to like, make sure we play properly tonight like we always did.

LUKE: Remember how serious we used to get? Like we'd get so into it.

BENNY: Remember that time no-one told Willa the game was over, and she still thought we were playing at school weeks later, and we all thought she hated us because she was being so hostile?

WILLA: I don't know why everyone else just assumed the game ended when we left the room. Like it was a psychological game.

LUKE: You are so cute 'cause like you're kinda smart but then you do stuff like that and it's like WOW. Anyway, sign the book.

WILLA: I still think we shouldn't mess with the book.

KAT: Well, it's done now, Willa.

LUKE: Actually, I'm going to buy into the idea that the book has all this power. Willa is right. The book has feelings. That girl shit will keep us accountable.

KAT: How is that 'girl shit'?

WILLA: Bad shit happens to people all the time when they mess with this stuff.

KAT: How is like the supernatural 'girl shit', tell me?

LUKE: I don't know witches are like always chicks.

TILLY: I mean, I believe in spirits and stuff but like …

JEREMY: Nah, Harry Potter is a dude.

KAT: Harry Potter IS a dude. So magic isn't 'girl shit'.

WILLA: [*to* TILLY] Exactly aren't we like tempting fate?

GWEN: I mean we are just using it to hold us accountable. We aren't calling on spirits.

TILLY: Harry Potter doesn't count anymore, by the way.

WILLA: I want to do shit to make this like a safe space anyway. Like sanctify it.

LUKE: Because you think this place is haunted?

BENNY: Wait why doesn't Harry Potter count?

GWEN: [*to* WILLA] What?

WILLA: What? No! Gwen, no. I just—I'm not saying this has anything to do with your dad. I don't like to mess with this stuff. Stuff with history, you know?

TILLY: [*to* BENNY] 'Cause y'know, the whole thing?

GWEN: You know what? I don't care. I just want to play the game. So do whatever you need.

WILLA: Great! Luke, go get some mirrors.

KAT: Hang on what, so now we just can't even like Harry Potter?

LUKE: Wait, why do I have to get mirrors?

TILLY: Not unless you hate the LGBTQI community.

GWEN: I actually agree with Luke, magic is for girls, like historically at least.

LUKE: Thank you!

WILLA: Luke get the mirrors please!

JEREMY: What are you talking about, Gwen, you think that like Japanese rituals were only done by women, like Mayan shit and voodoo?

KAT: That's bullshit, what about all the gay people who love Harry Potter? It's like so reductive it misses the point.

GWEN: Forget it. It doesn't matter.

WILLA: Put them all around the room, like find as many as you can.

BENNY: I'm gay and I give you permission to like Harry Potter if you want.

TILLY: You can't do that.

BENNY: Ooo but I did.

LUKE: You have to tell my why I'm doing this.

WILLA: They scare away evil spirits.

JEREMY: No Gwen, you said magic was like feminine or some shit and that's just historically not a fact.

GWEN: Why are you yelling at me?

LUKE: How do mirrors do that, stupid?

KAT: Wait, John Lennon was like abusive, wasn't he? I don't see anyone rushing to cancel The Beatles.

BENNY: Yeah, if we cancelled all the abusive people we'd have like no art.

KAT: No good art.

JEREMY: Seriously. I'm not even allowed to disagree with you anymore?

WILLA: I'm surprised you don't get a fright every time you look in a mirror.

LUKE: [*looking in mirror*] I'm surprised I haven't given myself a boner.

GWEN: I just meant that like, women have historically been like disempowered by society and …

KAT: Women aren't the only people who have been oppressed.

TILLY: Yeah exactly, like gay people and trans people.

GWEN: I'm not saying that.

KAT: Okay cool but like what are you saying?

BENNY: So, you are saying you can never like anything if the person who made it is a dick?

GWEN: No.

BENNY: I was talking to Tilly.

GWEN: Oh, well I was saying that like, witchcraft was—

WILLA: Guys where is the salt?

TILLY: Well, you are like directly funding abuse so yeah pretty much. Also, there are plenty of people who make great art without being like. Toxic.

Pause.

JEREMY: Gandalf.

LUKE: BOOM!

GWEN: Yeah, but he's made up.

WILLA: Luke, that's not enough mirrors.

JEREMY: Oh, I am sorry, I didn't realise we were only talking about all those 'real' magic people, my bad.

LUKE: Sorry boss. How many do we need?

GWEN: Jeremy.

WILLA: Just get more.

JEREMY: You don't have to be magic to do magic—

BENNY: What about Kanye?

GWEN: Okay fine, Jeremy—

JEREMY: —that's all I'm saying.

LUKE: I love Kanye.

GWEN: Whatever, you are right, okay?

KAT: BPD King.

TILLY: What about Kanye?

LUKE: Can we play the game already?

> WILLA *starts spreading salt around the floor.*

WILLA: This is sea salt; I don't know if that matters.

BENNY: You are saying we can't separate the art from the artist, but what about mental health?

TILLY: Wait. I'm not even going to dignify that.

LUKE: Should we pray or something, Wils?

TILLY: Are you saying all mentally ill people are abusive?

KAT: [*to* LUKE] I thought you weren't religious.

LUKE: I'm not. But I can hear my nonna's voice in my head. She wants me to pray.

WILLA: Luke, can you please get another mirror?

TILLY: There are always spirits around you just can't see them.

BENNY: I mean if there were going to be spirits anywhere …

WILLA: Oh my God. I really don't want to see a spirit.

JEREMY: What do you mean there are always spirits around?

LUKE: Gwen, where do I look for a mirror? One that I can pick up.

TILLY: You know. Spirits are like memories. They just float in and out.

GWEN: Upstairs.

> LUKE *walks upstairs and gestures for* BENNY *to help him.* BENNY *expresses his dissatisfaction but follows.*

JEREMY: Okay, so memories are always around, that's a bit different, Tilly.

TILLY: Yeah, but a spirit is like a memory that isn't attached to you. It's attached to something else like a place or an object.

GWEN: Tilly knows all about this stuff. She did a tarot card reading for me and it was crazy accurate.

JEREMY: Memories aren't possible outside of consciousness.

WILLA: I got a tarot reading on TikTok and it was pretty accurate.

TILLY: There's like collective consciousness. And like there are theories that the whole universe has consciousness.

WILLA: But it was based on the algorithm, so I don't know how it works.

KAT: So, you are saying that like a wall can have a memory?

TILLY: Pretty much.

GWEN: I guess if there weren't any hashtags that's sort of magic.

LUKE *and* BENNY *walk in holding big mirrors.*

LUKE: That's not magic, that's the Chinese.

GWEN: What are you *talking* about?

JEREMY: But you don't seriously believe that Tilly? Like it's just for fun right?

TILLY: No, I totally believe it.

LUKE: Um, the Chinese own TikTok, and they use it to listen to you.

JEREMY: That's insane, you realise that, right?

TILLY: No, it's not.

WILLA: Yeah, but she like shuffled the deck, the Chinese don't control that.

KAT: Why are you getting so defensive, Jeremy?

JEREMY: I don't like shit like this. It's a lie. It gives people a false sense of like security and certainty.

LUKE: No, but the Chinese listen to the content, and they know about the shit you like, so it probably just matched.

KAT: How is that any different from religion?

JEREMY: I don't like religion either.

WILLA: So, you are saying they are like always listening to me?

GWEN: I mean that's kind of like everything in a way.

JEREMY: No, not at all. What are you talking about?

GWEN: Babe, tone. I'm just saying that there are lots of things that have their own little worlds with their own little rules which make them feel good.

BENNY: Isn't that kind of racist?

JEREMY: No, this is different.

LUKE: Nah, it's awesome. I can't wait until they can implant a chip in my brain.

KAT: How, Jer?

GWEN: Honestly Kat, don't bother, he's in a mood.

JEREMY: What are the mirrors for?

LUKE: So, we can SEE the spirits apparently.

BENNY: Oh, wait I get it. Instagram doesn't have a brain, but it has memories.

GWEN: No, you can't look in the mirrors.

LUKE: Then why did we bring them down here??

WILLA: Because we need them! You never listen!

BENNY: So, like the earth has an algorithm?

LUKE: No, that's not what I meant at all.

BENNY: Not you.

TILLY: It's kind of like, you know like old school VHS, how people would like tape the TV onto the thing. It's like that. It's called stone taping.

KAT: So, you are saying the walls are taping us?

LUKE: [*sarcastically*] There are people in the walls?

JEREMY: Can we play the game already?

GWEN: We're interested, Til. Can you shut up, Luke?

TILLY: It's not that there are people in the walls. It's like when something big happens, or if something has a particularly big impact, it leaves a mark. In the same way something or someone can leave a mark on you.

BENNY: [*to* WILLA] So what does the salt do?

WILLA: It cleanses.

JEREMY: Of course. Does it stop the ground taping us?

TILLY: That's not how it works. It's not. It has to be like significant. It's not like everything gets recorded. Like it needs to be charged because it's all about energy.

WILLA: No-one disturb the salt, okay?

GWEN: Which is like why that forest you were telling me about in Japan is haunted, right, Til?

LUKE: The Aokigahara forest?

JEREMY: Do NOT encourage them.

KAT: Have you appropriately secured the venue, Miss Willa?

BENNY: The whadda whadda forest?

WILLA: No, I need everyone's phones. Technology is something they can manipulate.

LUKE: I saw a YouTube video. It's the most popular suicide …

He trails off looking at GWEN *and* TILLY. *Others copy him.*

JEREMY: Um, destination in the world. It's just like a creepy forest.

BENNY: I hate nature, it's so ick.

WILLA: Give me your phone.

BENNY: What? No way.

WILLA: Yes way, I'm putting our phones away until we are done with the game so they can't be used against us.

KAT: What do you really think, Jer? Be honest. You don't believe in ghosts?

JEREMY: I think … the mind is very powerful. People underestimate it.

WILLA: Phones please. Come on.

LUKE: Let's just give her our phones so we can get on with it, who cares.

JEREMY: Our brains recognise patterns and have instincts. And we don't always know we are doing it. And I think that ignorance makes people believe this shit.

TILLY: It's not shit.

JEREMY: Your brain controls everything, your hearing, sight, touch, smell, body temperature, your emotions. If you convince your brain that it is seeing something or hearing something. Well, it's going to see or hear that thing.

BENNY: Wow, what an absolute vibe-killer.

WILLA: Gwen, do you have a safe?

GWEN: What? Why?

WILLA: For the phones, they can't be here.

GWEN: Just … give them to me.

GWEN *takes the phones upstairs.*

KAT: What about when you know something isn't real, but you see it anyway?

JEREMY: I don't think it's like our conscious selves doing it. That's my point, it's like all happening beneath the surface.

TILLY: Cool, so there's literally no way for us to prove you wrong.

JEREMY: I'm not saying it to be a dick, I just think there's a scientific explanation.

TILLY: Science will always come up with an explanation … if it's the right one though? Who knows?

JEREMY: So, all scientists are liars, and the world is ruled by spiritual forces.

GWEN *comes back into the room.*

GWEN: I don't care if there are spirits or if they are real or it's conscious or whatever. I just want to have some fun.

TILLY: It is true.

WILLA: [*whispering*] I believe you. My dead dog visited me once in the middle of the night, it was so scary.

GWEN: Can you write your name already? I want to play.

LUKE: Til, when did you first realise you had these powers?

TILLY: You can't help yourself, can you?

WILLA: I'm going to do it, but I just—

LUKE: Willa, commme onnn.

WILLA: Okay!

LUKE: Oh, you are super-fucked now. For like life.

TILLY: God you are cynical.

LUKE: I'm not being cynical.

WILLA: Yes, you are.

LUKE: Um, how?

GWEN: You are making fun and asking all these questions.

LUKE: I'm interested—

WILLA: —yeah but—

LUKE: —being curious.

KAT: —you aren't asking 'cause your curious, you are asking because you are trying to prove it like wrong.

LUKE: I swear on my life, I am trying to have an open mind.

GWEN: [*to* LUKE] You can't laugh.

LUKE: I won't laugh.

LUKE *snorts.*

WILLA: Stop it.

LUKE: I'm sorry. Gee.

JEREMY: Yeah, Luke, stop.

LUKE: Hey Jer, I'm going to tell everyone about this.

TILLY: Hey Google, turn down the lights.

The lights dim.

WILLA: Holy fuck.

LUKE: Is that necessary?

TILLY: Who wants to go first?

> *Various hushes.* LUKE *stares into the mirror behind* GWEN *he looks horrified.* GWEN *turns to look.*

WILLA: You're not supposed to look in the mirrors!

JEREMY: Yeah babe!

LUKE: Yeah babe, don't look in the mirror.

GWEN: It was Luke, he scared me.

JEREMY: [*into the mirror at* LUKE] Boo!

LUKE: Ah!

BENNY: It is actually impossible for me not to look.

TILLY: I've noticed.

BENNY: Like I'm trying but I am also serving tonight. Like I almost don't recognise myself.

KAT: Gagged.

WILLA: Sometimes I look in the mirror for like so long that I forget I am me. Like I full-on disassociate.

GWEN: Guys, focus.

KAT: Ambience.

WILLA: Shhh.

TILLY: Who is asking first?

KAT: I'll go.

> *She gestures for* BENNY *to come closer and thinks for a moment.* NICOLE *walks through the door and freezes when she catches* GWEN*'s eye.*

JEREMY: Oh shit.

KAT: What?

NICOLE: Hi.

> WILLA *gasps.*

GWEN: What are you doing here?

NICOLE: Benny texted me.

KAT: You did not.

NICOLE: He said you invited me.

GWEN: Benny.

BENNY: Didn't you say that? Weird.

NICOLE: I'll go.

GWEN: No stop.

NICOLE: No, this was stupid.

GWEN: Wait.

    Pause.

NICOLE: I—I don't know what you want me to say.

GWEN: I don't know what I want you to say either.

TILLY: Bit late for you to say anything now.

GWEN: Tilly can you just—

JEREMY: Maybe we should …

GWEN: You walked in that door pretty easy.

NICOLE: It was really hard actually.

    Pause.

  Um … I did want to, well I hoped that maybe, I could talk to you privately at some point to just like, clear the air.

GWEN: I mean you have my number; you know where I live, I've always been very accessible to you. I'm not the one who fell off the face of the earth.

NICOLE: Right. Yeah. I did want to reach out, like a lot.

GWEN: But you didn't.

NICOLE: No. I—I guess I—It's kind of—

GWEN: Just—You're here now just stay. You don't need to do all—that.

NICOLE: Are you sure?

GWEN: Just sit down.

WILLA: Yay! We're playing Paranoia. Sit here.

LUKE: Damn I thought there was going to be a fight.

BENNY: My cousin goes to your new school, Nicole.

WILLA: I've missed you! Do you know the game?

JEREMY: [*to* TILLY] Are you okay with her being here?

NICOLE: Yeah, I think I played it at Bec's once.

KAT: Yeah so, we are playing paranoia.

TILLY: Don't really have a choice.

BENNY: Sounds like some real fucked-up people go there.

NICOLE: Yeah.

JEREMY: Just talk to Gwen.

KAT: Oh, you need to write your name in the book.

NICOLE: Okay.

WILLA: It's like, our way of keeping ourselves honest. For science, you know?

NICOLE: What's the book?

LUKE: It's Mr Michaels' last book, he didn't publish it.

TILLY *gets up and walks toward the bar.*

NICOLE: What?

GWEN: [*to* TILLY] Where are you going?

LUKE: Yeah so, we wrote our names in it to like honour our part in his work.

TILLY: To take the edge off.

BENNY: And now we are going to play Paranoia because the book is like on paranoia, to like honour him.

LUKE: Oh shit, Til. Good idea. Get me one too.

JEREMY: It's a one-last-hurrah type of thing.

GWEN: Tilly, not tonight.

NICOLE: Are you crazy?

WILLA: That's why we are playing Paranoia too 'cause we thought it was like what we used to do.

NICOLE: Have you guys even read it?

KAT: Yeah, reading a book is our idea of a wild Saturday night.

LUKE: That's not the point, it's the vibe of the thing.

GWEN: It's fine, it's already done.

NICOLE: I'm not doing that.

LUKE: Come on.

NICOLE: That is inviting bad shit to happen.

BENNY: It's just a book.

NICOLE: No, things have energy in them.

JEREMY: Not this again.

WILLA: It's okay, I like fixed the room.

NICOLE: I think that's fucked up.

TILLY: Well, we signed it, so I guess we're fucked up too.

NICOLE: There are certain things you should just have some respect for.

GWEN: Like the respect you had for me?

NICOLE: Gwen.

GWEN: No seriously. I was going to be chill. But was that you showing me respect that day?

NICOLE: I should go.

GWEN: Or the day after? Or the day after that?

WILLA: Nicole.

NICOLE: No.

GWEN: Just say sorry!

NICOLE: I'm going to go.

KAT: Nicole.

GWEN: Am I being crazy? Is that a crazy thing to ask for?

NICOLE: I am sorry! I am. Okay?

GWEN: Mean it.

NICOLE: I do.

> GWEN *scoffs.*

You think I wanted to walk back in here? Into *this* room? I came to say I am sorry. And, I don't know, explain.

GWEN: I don't believe you.

NICOLE: I am!

GWEN: I don't believe you.

NICOLE: I am so so so sorry for walking out on you that day. My body just, I didn't mean to. I saw him and, I don't know, And I'm sorry for dropping off.

GWEN: Not picking up calls, replying to texts, changing schools?

NICOLE: Yes Gwen, I'm sorry. God, I didn't want to do this in front of people.

GWEN: Oh, poor baby.

NICOLE: You know what I'm really sorry about Gwen? I'm really fucking sorry that I walked home from school with you that day and walked into this house and saw what I saw.

GWEN: Yeah, I'm sorry too.

NICOLE: I wish I wasn't with you. Maybe if I wasn't I could have been there for you after. But I am here now.

TILLY: Write your name in the book, Nicole.

NICOLE: Wha—No I've already said …

LUKE: If she doesn't put her name in the book she can't play.

WILLA: No, don't be a dick.

LUKE: That's the rules.

WILLA: So stupid.

KAT: That's how we are keeping ourselves honest.

GWEN: Write your name, Nicole.

NICOLE: I don't want to.

GWEN: Write your name in the book or leave.

BENNY: [*under his breath*] Drammmaaaa.

GWEN: It's a book. I am not asking for much.

NICOLE: This is … insane like literally traumatising.

GWEN: No, it's pen and paper.

LUKE: What? You think it's like Jumanji or something?

WILLA: Nic we are all here together, like it will be totally fine.

GWEN: Please.

NICOLE: Okay.

BENNY: Yes.

WILLA: We're playing the game; we're playing the game. Eee. I'm so excited.

LUKE: Here we go.

JEREMY: Okay, question.

GWEN: Who asked the last one?

JEREMY: Wait I've got a fun one.

He whispers in GWEN*'s ear.*

GWEN: Kat.

The coin is flipped, and it lands on heads.

KAT: Okay. What was it?

GWEN: Who is the most likely to stalk their ex?

KAT: Ummm.

GWEN: You went a bit nuts with Alex.

KAT: I didn't stalk him.

GWEN: Yes, you did.

KAT: No, I was persistent in my attempts to understand why he dumped me.

JEREMY: Ah, of course.

KAT: And once I was satisfied, I completely dropped it.

NICOLE: A year later.

KAT: Yeah, good research takes time.

WILLA: Didn't you like wait outside his house?

KAT: Yes, I did, but he never saw me so that doesn't count.

TILLY: Yes, it does.

KAT: No, stalking means that someone is like scared, Alex literally didn't even know I was there.

LUKE: That's psycho logic.

KAT: You guys clearly don't remember Jeremy after the Becca thing.

GWEN: I had forgot about that!

JEREMY: That was like Year 9.

KAT: You pined.

JEREMY: We barely even kissed!

WILLA: Didn't you write her a letter and like give it to her mum?

JEREMY: Yeah, she wouldn't talk to me.

KAT: See, that's stalking.

LUKE: I don't get either of you, gotta love em and leave em.

TILLY: Tell us more about how well that is working for you Luke.

KAT: Oh, got him.

LUKE: Okay next question. Let's ask … Nicole.

> LUKE *whispers in* NICOLE'*s ear.*

NICOLE: Gwen.

> *A coin is flipped, it lands on heads.*

Who is most likely to be famous.

GWEN: Why me?

NICOLE: Because, I don't know, you're perfect.

JEREMY: She's sucking up to you.

NICOLE: No, I'm not. I think a lot of people would want to be like Gwen. In school, the way people would look at her, it's like she was sunshine.

LUKE: Alright, lesbian.

WILLA: Wow, that's like really poetic.

GWEN: She wants to be a writer, remember?

LUKE: How do you even become a writer? Like do you go to uni or do you just like … start writing.

NICOLE: I'm going to uni. But I'm technically already published.

JEREMY: No shit!

TILLY: Where?

NICOLE: Just an essay for a competition. I wrote about when Mr Morrison tried to teach us that Jupiter was bigger than the sun. And put me in detention for pushing back.

KAT: Mr Morrison was such a fucking retard.

NICOLE: Yeah, and then at the space museum the astroguy was like 'obviously the sun is bigger' and everyone just looked at him and then looked at me. And he had to apologise to me. He was so mad.

JEREMY: That's crazy, that was you?

LUKE: Damn.

WILLA: I thought that happened to Sarah Marks?

NICOLE: No, it was definitely me.

WILLA: Are you sure?

NICOLE: Yeah, I'm positive.

WILLA: No, it can't have been you, you weren't in that class.

NICOLE: It was.

LUKE: Weren't you in our science class though, with Ms Phillps?

WILLA: Hang on I'll message—oh shit no phones.

NICOLE: I swear on my life, it was me.

WILLA: [*putting hands up*] Okay.

    Pause.

BENNY: Look, I'll admit that there is a universe where Gwen blows up as a mummy home-decor blogger, but you had way better choices. Sorry Gwen.

GWEN: I don't want to be famous.

LUKE: Yeah, my money would have been on Willa.

NICOLE: I feel like everyone wants to be famous to be fair.

WILLA: Me?

TILLY: You just have that 'it' girl look.

KAT: No Nic, it's more that everyone already acts like they are famous.

WILLA: I don't even use socials though.

BENNY: Yes, you do, you're on Snap.

KAT: People don't even have personalities anymore; they just have platforms and identities.

WILLA: Yeah, you don't really influence on snap chat.

BENNY: Um that's cap. Your snapchats are art.

NICOLE: What does that even mean, Kat?

JEREMY: Sorry 'influencing' isn't art.

BENNY: No, I think posting can be art.

KAT: I can tell what platform every person in this room prefers.

JEREMY: Absolutely not.

BENNY: I think anything can be art.

JEREMY: This whole thing has been, like, who is the most likely to get famous for nothing. It's gross.

TILLY: People can have personalities and use the internet, Kat.

BENNY: Haven't you ever read a post on Reddit or something that is just so good it feels like a work of art.

LUKE: Yes, the potato guy. SO good.

KAT: Did all your little trauma make you Tumblr famous, Til? Do your problems get you clicks?

JEREMY: That's a story, not art.

BENNY: It's about how you tell the story, that's all influencing is.

TILLY: You can't speak to me like that.

GWEN: I get where Jeremy is coming from though 'cause it feels like it's just about having money.

KAT: Just proving a point.

BENNY: No, you just have to look like you have money. That's the secret.

JEREMY: That's so fucked up.

BENNY: Gotta keep up appearances.

KAT: Bleak.

BENNY: I think we've established that the right answer was me, as I am clearly the only one who understands fame.

WILLA: Okay, I want to answer one.

> BENNY *whispers in* WILLA's *ear.*

Jeremy.

JEREMY: Me? Flip the coin.

> *The coin is flipped, it lands on heads.*

BENNY: Oh no …

KAT: You have to say.

LUKE: Who has the second biggest dick in the room?

BENNY: After me.

WILLA: I'm sorry Jeremy.

LUKE: Who has the third biggest dick.

TILLY: What was the actual question?

NICOLE: Hurry up.

GWEN: Those are the rules, babe.

WILLA: Who's the most likely to end up living on minimum wage?

GWEN: Wait, why Jeremy?

KAT: Yeah, like for real it's gotta be Luke.

LUKE: No, come on, what about Benny?

BENNY: I have a little something called talent.

KAT: He's a star.

BENNY: I'm a money magnet. Money will just come to me.

LUKE: How?

BENNY: I will manifest it.

LUKE: Get off it.

BENNY: I'm one viral thirst trap away from being a gay icon.

WILLA: Yeah.

BENNY: So, I won't be on the dole, I am just currently pre-rich.

WILLA: And I mean Jeremy is the only one of us not going to uni.

GWEN: What?

NICOLE: Ha ha.

> *Pause.*

Oh.

JEREMY: You told her?

> *Silence.*

WILLA: Oh shit.

GWEN: What does that mean? You told her.

WILLA: I'm sorry.

LUKE: I just—WILLA!

WILLA: I'm SORRY.

BENNY: No way.

KAT: Oh my God.

WILLA: Jer, I didn't know people didn't know.

KAT: Oh my God, I thought you were joking but you're serious.

GWEN: I'm sorry, someone needs to tell me what's happening right now.

TILLY: Let's keep playing. Who's flipping the coin next?

KAT: No no no no we are not done here. Aren't you starting uni like next week?

LUKE: It's nothing. We should move on.

KAT: It's not nothing. This is the game!

WILLA: Just leave it.

KAT: Wha—No!

NICOLE: I don't think this is something we all need to be involved in.

BENNY: I don't want to be that guy but technically …

WILLA: This isn't funny, Benny. It's serious.

GWEN: Jeremy.

BENNY: You have to explain Jeremy, that's kind of part of it.

GWEN: What the fuck is going on?

BENNY: The rules.

NICOLE: This isn't part of the game.

TILLY: Maybe talk about it later?

GWEN: No, Jeremy. You can't just not address that. Tell me what is going on. Now!

JEREMY: I failed, are you fucking happy?

GWEN: Failed what?

JEREMY: Failed school, I didn't pass.

KAT: Shiiit.

BENNY: No way. Like you, you totally failed not just got a bad score?

LUKE: Willa, I am so pissed at you.

GWEN: You—we studied together …

LUKE: It's his mum, he—

JEREMY: Shut up!

LUKE: I'm defending you, bro. Don't yell at me.

JEREMY: I don't need to be defended.

TILLY: He doesn't want to talk about her.

LUKE: But he's not saying anything.

WILLA: Wait, I mean are sure you even failed, like how do you know?

JEREMY: I know.

GWEN: But that means you lied about getting into uni?

JEREMY: Yes.

GWEN: And you just, you made plans with me, you let me make all of these plans knowing you were lying?

JEREMY: It's not about you.

GWEN: It kind of is about me.

WILLA: Gwen.

GWEN: No, this is so wrong, Jeremy. We signed a lease agreement. I've been packing my stuff up.

JEREMY: It's *not* about you.

GWEN: It IS about me! Were you even planning on coming with me?

NICOLE: Guys let's just give him some space, like we don't all need to be probing him on how he fucked his life up.

JEREMY: You never asked me if I wanted to go, you just decided.

KAT: He hasn't fucked up his life, Nic.

NICOLE: Um, failing is a pretty big deal.

GWEN: [*to* JEREMY] No, we talked about it a lot actually.

JEREMY: Did we?

KAT: He hasn't fucked up his life, his life's fucked, that's different.

GWEN: Yes, we did.

JEREMY: And you heard in all those conversations that I wanted to leave my dying mum and move to another state?

NICOLE: No, actually a lot of people can cope under pressure.

KAT: You really want to go there, Nicole?

GWEN: You *told* me you wanted to go to Melbourne.

JEREMY: No, you heard that. Why would I want that?

GWEN: Why didn't you say you wanted to stay? That you needed help?

JEREMY: I shouldn't have to tell you that I want to be with my mum.

GWEN: I can only go off what you tell me, Jeremy, and you told me you wanted to go.

JEREMY: Well, I don't want to go! I don't want to leave. I don't give a fuck about school. I don't give a fuck about uni. I don't give a fuck about your plans or your feelings.

KAT: Whoa.

JEREMY: Can we just stop talking about this please?

> *Pause.*

This is a stupid fucking game. I'm getting a drink.

> *Long silence. Some people look at each other, some avoid eye contact.*

WILLA: Luke hangs pictures of dead dictators on his walls.

NICOLE: Wait, what?

GWEN: Do you actually?

LUKE: Yeah.

NICOLE: Like Stalin and Pol Pot and shit?

LUKE: Yeah, I've got like twenty.

NICOLE: Why the fuck are you like celebrating dictators?

LUKE: I'm not celebrating anything.

BENNY: Ummmmmmm …

LUKE: It's just like a reminder.

GWEN: Of what?

LUKE: Of like, how much evil there is in the world just like around. And like how evil one person can become.

KAT: You wanna be evil?

LUKE: No, not really.

BENNY: Oh, well that's reassuring at least—

TILLY: Are all dictators evil?

BENNY: —I like how you said it with so much enthusiasm.

GWEN: Ah yeah, that's kinda the whole point.

WILLA: I don't think so.

LUKE: I just like, don't think of it like that.

NICOLE: What do you mean you don't think so?

WILLA: I watched this YouTube video about Gaddafi, like the Libyan guy—

TILLY: Yeah.

BENNY: Is this …

KAT: Gaddafi.

BENNY: —Gaddafi on your wall?

WILLA: —and like he actually seemed like a pretty good guy.

LUKE: Yeah, Gaddafi's up there.

NICOLE: Um I'm pretty sure he wasn't a good guy.

WILLA: No, I mean like, I don't think you can just trust the media you have to like look for both sides.

BENNY: Hang on, are we positive this is one of *those* things?

KAT: Wait how did you even find that video, Will?

WILLA: I fell asleep and when I woke up my YouTube had been like autoplaying, so I just like watched it.

GWEN: What do you even mean, look for both sides? I don't think there are two sides to what was happening in Libya.

KAT: What *was* happening in Libya exactly Gwen?

BENNY: Fucked if I know.

WILLA: Yeah, I think there are lots of sides.

BENNY: Wait, what did the video say?

WILLA: Just like he did lots of good things like he improved like how well people could read and how much money they had.

NICOLE: Isn't that they guy who got like dragged through the streets and raped and shit?

WILLA: Yeah, it was like really fucking sad.

GWEN: Um, not if you were Libyan.

WILLA: You don't know that.

GWEN: Pretty sure I do. Pretty sure you don't kill someone without a good reason.

WILLA: I am pretty sure being publicly tortured and murdered is sad no matter what.

GWEN: That's just incorrect.

KAT: Get off it Gwen, we didn't even cover the Arab Spring in modern history. You don't have to pretend to be an expert every time you get offended.

WILLA: I'm just saying, everyone makes mistakes.

NICOLE: Ah of course, because our mistakes and Gaddafi's mistakes are totally the same.

WILLA: It's like not crazy that you could do something bad and think it was good.

NICOLE: Yeah, but we are talking scale?

GWEN: You're not going to say anything Jeremy?

WILLA: I'm just saying, don't throw stones in glass houses.

JEREMY: Nope.

TILLY: I read that when he died his house was full of like porn shit.

BENNY: Was I supposed to be reading about Gaddifi or …

GWEN: So, you are going to ruin the night because you got caught in a lie. Super-mature.

BENNY: 'Cause I just feel like everyone seems to like at least know who this guy is, and I literally know nothing about the man.

LUKE: I mean you guys get so spooked out by like that voodoo astrology shit and meanwhile there's like real fucking evil in the world. Like messed-up stuff.

BENNY: Kat said she would have killed the Jews in World War Two.

JEREMY: What?

KAT: That's not what I said.

GWEN: You can't say shit like that.

KAT: I didn't say that. I mean I said something similar.

WILLA: Jesus Christ.

KAT: But it was more of like a philosophical point.

LUKE: Oh, is this the Nazi thing again?

BENNY: Again?

LUKE: Yeah, she was going on about some cooked Hitler and groupthink thing at Joeys.

KAT: I don't know why you are acting like it's crazy. It's a pretty common-sense point.

JEREMY: Made in the most batshit crazy way.

KAT: Jeremy, you're just upset because you're basically the poster boy for Hitler Youth.

GWEN: Kat, oh my God, stop.

LUKE: I kind of see that, sorry dude.

KAT: The point I was making was that we all love to imagine that in the moment we would see things for what they are. That we wouldn't get swept up in it. That like we'd think critically, and we'd do the right thing no matter what we thought the costs were.

JEREMY: Yeah, I think we would.

KAT: No, we'd be Nazis.

LUKE: You are crazy for this.

KAT: And we'd think we were doing the right thing. And if you honestly think that's not the case then you're just deluded.

BENNY: We're deluded if we don't want to be Nazis?

GWEN: I feel like, most people know genocide is wrong.

KAT: Sure that makes sense, here, now. But like imagine every piece of news you get for years pushes one narrative. And you don't have any access to any other information. And it's telling you shit like you should be afraid, like bad things are going to happen. How do you see past that?

TILLY: You just do because it's like the right thing to do.

KAT: Okay, well, you like live in a free society now and you have access to all kinds of information. So, tell me all your *independent* thoughts, Gwen? The ones that go against the grain. The ones that cost you something.

NICOLE: My independent thought is it's not fucking cute to joke about the Holocaust.

KAT: How brave of you, Nicole, tell me about the Holocaust. Since you care. *So* much.

JEREMY: We all know about the Holocaust.

KAT: Do we? Wow!

GWEN: Yes, Kat.

KAT: I mean of course we know it was bad.

WILLA: It was fucking genocide.

NICOLE: Yeah, like pure evil.

KAT: Mmm genocides *are* pure evil.

JEREMY: Yes.

KAT: So, I am sure you have lots to say about Armenia, of course. And you can explain to me all the juicy details of genocides our government actually funds like the one happening in Yemen. Or what's going on in the Tigray. Or Myanmar?

NICOLE: That's not the point.

KAT: Actually, tell me about any genocide at all.

TILLY: You don't need to know all the details of something to know it's wrong.

KAT: The thing is, little Tilly. If I had used any other example, you'd have kept your mouth shut. And I think if you are going to be indignant about something, you better be able to back it up.

BENNY: Ow.

GWEN: [*whispering*] Then why didn't you use another example?

KAT: Excuse me?

GWEN: Why didn't you use another example, then?

KAT: Why don't you kill yourself?

WILLA: WHOA.

KAT: I asked you a question Gwen?

GWEN: Why the fuck would I kill myself?

NICOLE: Kat, that's a bit insensitive.

KAT: What?

> GWEN *looks at* TILLY *who looks very distressed.* KAT *realises what she's said.*

No, I mean, sorry I mean. Jesus. I didn't mean it like that.

GWEN: Tilly?

>TILLY *does not respond.*

KAT: Tilly, I'm sorry I wasn't thinking about your dad I just—My point was just—

JEREMY: I think that's enough.

KAT: We do things because that's what everyone else is doing. Like sometimes we stay at a party even though we are having a bad time. Just because that's what's done. That is what everyone is doing. They are staying. We do what the people around us do. What they say is the okay thing to do. Doesn't matter how shit of time you are having! And that's why most of us don't kill ourselves even though our lives are shitty. You don't leave because like nobody else is leaving.

>*No-one says anything.*

TILLY: Some people leave.

>TILLY *walks away from the group.*

JEREMY: Good job.

>JEREMY *follows to comfort her, perhaps a little too intimately.*

KAT: Come on, I was making a philosophical point.

GWEN: You never know when to stop making philosophical points, Kat.

WILLA: Kat you should tone it down just a little. I mean it's only been six months.

JEREMY: [*to* TILLY] You okay?

KAT: Oh, is that the rule, no-one explained to me when it was cool to talk about these things.

TILLY: She's right.

NICOLE: Yeah, 'cause you should just know.

JEREMY: No, she's not.

KAT: Oh, 'cause you always know how to behave.

TILLY: People aren't supposed to leave. But he did.

BENNY: I've heard some things about your behaviour, Nic.

JEREMY: He did.

TILLY: I just wish I could talk to him one more time.

JEREMY: I know.

>JEREMY *lifts* TILLY*'s chin and presses his forehead against hers.*

BENNY: Um what's going on?

JEREMY: Nothing.

BENNY: Very intimate nothing.

JEREMY: She's upset, alright.

NICOLE: Jeremy, that's a bit …

JEREMY: What?

NICOLE: Nothing. I'm really sorry about your mum by the way. My mum told me it's been hard the last couple of months.

JEREMY: [*yelling*] Can we just play the fucking game?

KAT: Whoa.

JEREMY: Luke.

LUKE: Bro, I seriously didn't mean to.

JEREMY: We are playing.

LUKE: Yeah okay.

JEREMY: I've got a question.

> JEREMY *whispers a question in* LUKE'*s ear. It's clear from his face it's an intense question.*

LUKE: Um. Whoa.

JEREMY: Answer it.

> *Pause.*

BENNY: Pussy.

LUKE: We're not playing easy mode then.

JEREMY: Answer.

LUKE: Willa.

GWEN: Now flip the coin.

> *The coin is flipped, it lands on heads.*

LUKE: Who's the biggest slut here?

GWEN: LUKE.

LUKE: I mean, it's sort of a compliment.

WILLA: I can't believe you just said that.

LUKE: I see the way you look at me.

WILLA: Oh my God.

LUKE: JOKE, joke.

BENNY: Willa, outrage aside.

LUKE: It's mean but it's not rude.

WILLA: No, it is rude, I'm not a slut.

KAT: Ha, come on!

NICOLE: Kat! Stop.

WILLA: No, I'm not a slut.

KAT: Willa, look at me and say that with a straight face.

WILLA: I'm not a slut.

GWEN: It's a shitty way to phrase it.

WILLA: It doesn't matter how it's phrased.

NICOLE: No that's not what she means.

GWEN: No, I mean you are allowed to be sexual.

WILLA: Okay, what the fuck does that mean?

GWEN: I'm just saying you don't have to be this pure innocent thing like women used to have to be.

KAT: Stop being precious, you're the biggest slut here, and you know it. Don't get butthurt about a game.

WILLA: If I'm such a slut why have I never had sex then, Kat?

LUKE: Nah, that's cap.

GWEN: You've seriously never had sex?

WILLA: It's actually no-one's business.

LUKE: No, come on you can't just say something like that and then shut it down.

JEREMY: I didn't get to shut it down.

LUKE: Yeah, we have to be fair, all cards on the table.

WILLA: You actually don't have some right to my personal information.

GWEN: No, I think we were just surprised.

WILLA: Why? Because of the way I look?

BENNY: Well, a little bit, yeah.

WILLA: I don't know why everyone thinks they have an opinion about me all the freaking time.

KAT: Why don't you tell them who that selfie was actually for?

GWEN: Oh my God, Willa, who?

WILLA: Kat, don't.

KAT: Tell them!

WILLA: Kat.

KAT: Willa has a sugar daddy.

NICOLE: What?!

TILLY: Holy shit.

JEREMY: That's disgusting.

LUKE: Wait, I don't get it.

GWEN: She's joking, right?

BENNY: She texts and sends pictures, and he sends her money.

JEREMY: So, you actually are a slut then.

GWEN: Jeremy.

LUKE: What kind of pictures?

JEREMY: What do you think.

TILLY: Is that even legal?

BENNY: She's eighteen.

GWEN: Just.

KAT: He's like some old man.

LUKE: Wills, that's gross.

NICOLE: Do you actually like have sex?

LUKE: Not some wrinkly old man, that's foul.

WILLA: No! I—Kat.

KAT: What?

BENNY: Well then, she's not a slut right because she'd need to have sex?

TILLY: She didn't technically answer.

GWEN: Slut is a gross word. She's not a slut. It's just a word to make people feel bad.

KAT: She is whoring herself out for money maybe she should feel bad.

NICOLE: No, she's said she's a virgin. Right, Willa?

KAT: Like it makes a difference.

GWEN: Kat what is your actual problem tonight?

WILLA: I—

GWEN: You don't need to be ashamed about it, Will.

WILLA: I know that.

KAT: Absolutely you should be ashamed.

NICOLE: You mean not ashamed?

KAT: No, I mean she should be ashamed.

GWEN: What?

WILLA: Oh my God.

LUKE: [*to* JEREMY] Drinks?

JEREMY *nods and follows* LUKE *to cupboard.*

Why do they tell you alcohol percentage?

WILLA: [*to* KAT] Are you serious?

KAT: Shame is important?

LUKE: Why isn't all alcohol just like one hundred percent?

KAT: Shame is your mind's way of telling you what it doesn't want to be doing. What it knows it shouldn't be doing.

WILLA: Can you just not be here anymore?

GWEN: I think that's an absolutely fucked point of view.

KAT: Well, I think it's absolutely fucked to be prostituting yourself online.

WILLA: That's not what I'm doing.

NICOLE: Honestly Kat, who do you think you are?

WILLA: I am not ashamed.

NICOLE: Good for you.

KAT: Willa.

> KAT *sighs.*

You are. You are ashamed otherwise this wouldn't be such a big deal.

JEREMY: I think one-hundred-percent alcohol is like floor cleaner or some shit.

WILLA: It's a big deal because you embarrassed me.

KAT: You're embarrassed because you are ashamed of it!

WILLA: No, I am embarrassed because it was a private thing.

KAT: Which you kept private because you were ashamed.

LUKE: So, if floor cleaner is one hundred percent why don't we just find some of that?

GWEN: Luke no, that will literally fucking kill you.

KAT: I am your friend. And I am telling you to listen to yourself.

WILLA: My friend? Is that a joke?

JEREMY: I think that's a myth. I think you can drink it, but you have to have less.

GWEN: [*to* JEREMY] Can you please not drink fucking floor cleaner?

WILLA: You promise me you won't say anything and then literally the first opportunity you get—

LUKE: I'm going to google it.

NICOLE: You don't need to google it.

LUKE: I am going to google it.

KAT: Wills, I would not care if you slept with every person you made eye contact with if I thought it made you happy and that, I don't know, that it was like who you really were.

WILLA: You know what? Fuck you. Fuck all of you.

NICOLE: Hey what did I do?

WILLA: You know what I like it.

KAT: What?

WILLA: Being objectified.

KAT: You like being paid for?

WILLA: No, being admired. The more they admire you, the more they want your approval. I'm the one with the power. He doesn't have a hold of me, I have a hold of him.

KAT: For now.

> *Silence.*

WILLA: I don't need any of this. You don't know me.

JEREMY: There's cleaner here bro, but I don't know.

KAT: I know everything about you.

LUKE: Jer, what did you say? I couldn't hear you over the women.

NICOLE: [*to* LUKE] Seriously?

WILLA: I'm going to leave.

> WILLA *physically begins to leave before she appears to become stuck in space.*

GWEN: Okay, I understand.

WILLA: I'm just too—

JEREMY: I don't think we should drink this dude. There's like a warning—

KAT: [*to* WILLA] Don't. Don't do this.

JEREMY: [*to* KAT] Not going to.

WILLA: Seriously, leave me alone.

LUKE: Well, if we are not drinking floor cleaner, I am going to need more alcohol.

WILLA: I'm going to leave.

KAT: Then leave.

WILLA: I—

LUKE: What are you doing?

WILLA: I'm …

NICOLE: You good, Wils?

WILLA: I feel like really weird.

GWEN: Like you're going to vom?

WILLA: No like I'm—

GWEN: Hang on, let me get you an apple.

WILLA: I think I'm going to lie down.

WILLA *lies down on the floor.*

KAT: Ummm.

GWEN: Eat this. [*To* KAT] Make her eat this.

WILLA: I just—I think I'm going to stay.

Both boys stand with keys and wallet in hand, not moving

GWEN: Yeah, your blood sugar is probably low.

BENNY: I know you are sick, but you look amazing. It's giving Coppola.

KAT: Um, are you guys going?

LUKE: Yeah, for sure.

BENNY: The floor is working for you.

WILLA: Thanks babe.

The other girls look up and see the boys frozen in space.

GWEN: What are you doing?

JEREMY: Going to get some drinks.

NICOLE: Yeah, but you're like not.

LUKE: Yeah, but like … we're—

NICOLE: What?

JEREMY *and* LUKE *clearly have a desire to move but do not.*

BENNY: Wait, is this performance art?

KAT: Guys, cut it out. Just go already.

JEREMY: I don't really feel like beer.

LUKE: Yeah same.

KAT: Why are you guys being such freaks?

JEREMY: We're not we just don't feel like beer. What's your problem?

LUKE: If you want something, get it yourself.

KAT: Give me the keys.

JEREMY: No, you're not driving my car.

KAT: Fine, I'll walk.

KAT *looks at the door but does not move.* BENNY *looks at* WILLA.

I'll wait for Willa to feel better.

TILLY: Oh, now you care about how she feels?

WILLA: I'm just tired.

BENNY: I know, sweetie.

NICOLE: She's just having a bit of a rest.

BENNY: No totally, women and the floor.

NICOLE: Not like that.

KAT: Exactly like that.

GWEN: We should probably move her.

LUKE: You know what Willa? I've thought about it. The sugar daddy thing is hot. Especially if you're a virgin.

GWEN: One, two, three.

> *They lift her but not very well and swing her onto the couch.*

WILLA: Thanks Luke.

JEREMY: Yeah, I mean we already knew you took thot photos so all we really learnt is that Kat can't be trusted.

GWEN: Just put her here.

NICOLE: I think we all just got excited, okay? You don't need to feel bad about anything, Wills.

KAT: Hang on, so no-one has left the house?

LUKE: No, but we are about to.

KAT: Cool, so what's stopping you?

LUKE: Nothing. [*To* JEREMY] You coming, bro?

JEREMY: Yep. Leggo.

> *They walk toward the door. There is a bang from above. They stop. There is tension in their bodies as they look to the door.*

GWEN: What are you freaks doing? Go!

> GWEN *goes to the door.* WILLA *gasps. She stops in her tracks.*

Um.

TILLY: I don't think we should leave the house.

NICOLE: There's no way, right?

> WILLA *sits up.*

WILLA: I don't think it wants us to leave.

JEREMY: What do you mean 'it'?

WILLA: The book.

BENNY: Like spirits?

LUKE: It's not the book.

WILLA: I told you guys we shouldn't mess with it.

GWEN: It's not the book.

WILLA: Oh, I wasn't saying it was your …

BENNY: FUCK what if we're dreaming?

JEREMY: What all at the same time?

BENNY: Oh.

JEREMY: Having the same dream?

BENNY: Um.

JEREMY: Talking to each other?

LUKE: Could be that one of us is asleep and the rest of us are just NPCs.

NICOLE: Wait so like, whichever one of us is dreaming is the one who exists?

BENNY: Well then, I'm the one who is dreaming.

GWEN: None of us are dreaming.

KAT: Well, I mean there would literally be no way for us to know, right?

WILLA: I cannot think about not being real.

JEREMY: We are all real, chill.

TILLY: Maybe we are like daydreaming, though.

JEREMY: Once again, that doesn't make sense because we wouldn't all be having the same dream.

TILLY: No, that's not what I meant.

JEREMY: Okay?

TILLY: Like let's say I tell you I heard something, and then you start hearing things …

JEREMY: Yeah.

TILLY: It's more that you are listening for something, than that something is making noise.

A sound from above makes everyone pause.

KAT: We are psyching each other out.

LUKE: One hundred percent.

BENNY: It's got to be our imagination, right?

WILLA: I don't know.

WILLA *accidentally knocks something off the table and screams.*

JEREMY: Willa, stop you are making it worse.

WILLA: I'm not trying to, I'm just freaked out.

GWEN: I don't think you should leave.

NICOLE: No neither.

LUKE: Okay, the girls have officially lost it.

KAT: I don't see you running out the door.

LUKE: What's your point?

KAT: I think you're low-key scared to leave the house.

LUKE: Bullshit.

KAT: Then why are you still here?

> *Pause.*

LUKE: Because I want to finish the game.

KAT: Really?

LUKE: Yeah, I was actually having fun until all that shit about Willa being a slut, but I think we learned from it.

JEREMY: You were having fun?

LUKE: Oh, sorry bro, I felt bad about your shit too. That's two mistakes we've learned from.

TILLY: Maybe we have to play.

BENNY: Yeah. Maybe we've like locked ourselves into the game.

WILLA: That's why we can't leave.

JEREMY: Okay no, we can leave.

> *He moves toward the door but stops.*

TILLY: [*to* WILLA] What do you think will happen if we leave?

NICOLE: I know it's kind of different, but my cousin Natalie played this game—it was like a spiritual game, sort of like hide and seek. But she played with some of her friends and two of them got scared and broke the rules.

WILLA: Oh shit.

NICOLE: Yeah, and like Nat says that all this bad shit happened to them for years and then they both died like super-young in freak accidents.

JEREMY: Oh, come on.

NICOLE: No, that actually happened. And like the girls who died even said that they thought the bad stuff that was happening was because of the game.

JEREMY: That's actually nonsense. Bad shit happens because bad shit happens, not because you pissed off some ghosts.

WILLA: Oh my God, remember Emma who like went crazy and left school in Year 9. Didn't someone say she got into contact with some evil spirit on camp when they did a séance?

NICOLE: Yes, I was in that room, everyone was screaming and crying, and we had to get the reverend to come and bless the room.

LUKE: You girls are nuts you know that, right?

TILLY: Then why don't you walk out the door, Luke?

> LUKE *laughs nervously and looks at the door.*

LUKE: Because I told you I want to play the game.

KAT: I don't know about the whole spirit pact thing, but we should at least play until we've all had our feelings hurt.

GWEN: Ha ha.

KAT: That's how the game works, right?

NICOLE: Seems to be how every game you play works, Kat.

WILLA: I'll second that.

NICOLE: Remember when Kat came up with that game where we all had to spread a rumour about someone.

BENNY: Who the fuck came up with this game?

LUKE: Someone who hated their friends.

TILLY: Okay. Who has a question?

> LUKE *flips the coin for fun.*

GWEN: Wait, flip the coin again.

LUKE: No-one has asked a question.

GWEN: Just flip it.

> *He flips the coin.*

Okay, flip it again.

> *He flips the coin.*

Again.

WILLA: Whaaaat?

GWEN: That's weird, right?

NICOLE: It's only landed on heads, right?

LUKE: Yeah.

GWEN: It should have landed on tails by now.

NICOLE: Maybe it's just the way he's flipping it?

WILLA: Let me try then.

BENNY: Fuck.

TILLY: Wait go again.

GWEN: That's WEIRD, right?

JEREMY: Maybe there is a problem with the coin.

BENNY: Is it one of those trick coins?

KAT: Gwen, are you trying to be funny?

GWEN: No.

KAT: Because that never works.

GWEN: No, it's a normal fucking coin from my wallet.

JEREMY: Flip it again.

LUKE: What—

GWEN: Okay.

LUKE: —the fuck.

NICOLE: Flip it slow, like you are really trying to get tails.

WILLA: How am I supposed to do that?

NICOLE: I don't know.

JEREMY: Can you get another coin?

LUKE: Hang on, I might have one in my wallet.

JEREMY: Here.

> JEREMY *gives the new coin over, and* WILLA *flips it.*

TILLY: Heads.

JEREMY: Go again, we have to break it in.

GWEN: It's a coin.

JEREMY: Just flip it again.

BENNY: Guess it wants us to say the questions.

JEREMY: It's a coin, it doesn't want.

BENNY: Well, something wants us to say the questions out loud.

> *There is loud sound,* WILLA *screams and hits* LUKE.

WILLA: Sorry.

LUKE: It's just the aircon, chill.

WILLA: Sorry, I'm—maybe we should play in another room.

LUKE: No, fuck that, let's just go. Someone ask a question. I'm grabbing a drink.

TILLY: I've got one.

TILLY *whispers in* BENNY*'s ear.*

BENNY: Luke.

Coin flips on heads.

JEREMY: Alright, let's hear it.

BENNY: Who's the biggest creep?

NICOLE: Ha!

LUKE: Why me?

JEREMY: Yeah.

TILLY: Who else?

LUKE: She sends pics of her feet to an old man!

WILLA: No, I don't!

LUKE: Sorry Wills I'm just—

GWEN: Technically, the old man is the creep.

LUKE: You're a good girl.

KAT: Good girl??

NICOLE: The behaviour is what's creepy …

LUKE: Wait, what do you even mean by creepy?

TILLY: You know, like creepy.

JEREMY: No.

TILLY: Like people talk.

NICOLE: So now everyone thinks you're creepy.

LUKE: Yeah, but what does that mean?

TILLY: Like a little dangerous, I guess.

BENNY: Michael Jackson was creepy.

KAT: Agreed.

GWEN: You're just a little rapey.

LUKE: Rapey?

NICOLE: Yeah.

KAT: Creepy is like when you don't know for sure, hey?

LUKE: What the fuck does that mean?

GWEN: Just that …

KAT: You think they might, but there isn't enough to know.

NICOLE: You've hooked up with a lot of girls.

LUKE: Yeah, hooked up, not raped.

NICOLE: Yeah, but like, people talk.

LUKE: About what?

WILLA: I think what she's trying to say is—

GWEN: —You don't talk to any of your exes.

LUKE: Yes, I do.

GWEN: No.

LUKE: Yes, I do. I talk to Jessica.

BENNY: But she's a bit of a slut.

TILLY: The thing is like, all your exes tell people to like stay away from you.

GWEN: It's talked about by the girls.

LUKE: Come on!

NICOLE: You have gone out with a lot of girls.

WILLA: That doesn't mean anything.

NICOLE: No, it does.

LUKE: I want to have some fun and date people casually so now I'm a rapist?

JEREMY: Jokes aside, Luke's a good guy.

LUKE: Just 'cause I don't want to settle down at seventeen.

KAT: I am so sick of this 'good guy' discourse.

JEREMY: Yeah, but he *is* a good guy.

KAT: So, it's just the rare 'bad guy' who rapes—But like most women will be assaulted.

GWEN: You lead people on, Luke.

JEREMY: Yeah Kat, I know it's hard to believe but not all men are evil.

LUKE: No, I don't!

KAT: So, it's just a few monsters out there attacking all the women.

JEREMY: Better than your version where it's all men.

KAT: No, I don't know why we all refuse to acknowledge it.

NICOLE: What?

> *The girls, excluding* WILLA, *physically align giving the scene the feeling of a prosecution.*

Alison.

LUKE: What about Alison?

GWEN: Becca's Snap.

KAT: She was like passed out and you were on top of her.

LUKE: I was carrying her.

NICOLE: Yeah, but you had been hooking up.

KAT: And then you forced yourself on her.

LUKE: When?

NICOLE: We saw it in the video.

JEREMY: In the background of a four-second video?

KAT: It was pretty clear.

LUKE: We didn't even have sex!

GWEN: Yeah right.

LUKE: We didn't!

TILLY: But you did like do stuff, like we heard …

NICOLE: Alison said she felt weird about it.

KAT: Did you ask for consent? Did she say yes?

LUKE: It wasn't like that.

KAT: So, rape then.

LUKE: No, we were both wasted.

BENNY: Come on Kat, you know that people can consent in other ways.

KAT: That's cope, so that men can say they were given mixed signals.

BENNY: What so every single time I touch someone or do something different I have to ask for consent?

KAT: Yes.

JEREMY: Come on.

KAT: That's actually not crazy.

BENNY: What if I am making out with someone and they like it and then, I don't know, I put my hand down their pants and they tell me no but then we go back to just making out. Did I assault them?

KAT: Yes.

BENNY: Then I guess everyone is a rapist, Kat, that is an impossible bar.

GWEN: I don't need to be asked but like, I need the person to look at my face.

WILLA: Yeah, I'd want them to give a shit about me.

KAT: I think we can all agree that Luke didn't give a shit about Alison.

LUKE: That's not true.

KAT: She was drunk, she couldn't consent.

JEREMY: I was drunk too.

WILLA: We were all drunk.

JEREMY: How come you don't think she took advantage of me?

KAT: You are bigger than her.

JEREMY: That's not—

LUKE: But I didn't do anything!

GWEN: [*to* JEREMY] Don't do that, don't be one of the boys.

KAT: Yes, you did.

JEREMY: What does that mean?

LUKE: Did she say that I did?

> *Pause.*

Did Alison say to you that I raped her?

KAT: She didn't need to.

JEREMY: Gwen?

LUKE: Oh well that's just … Why didn't you say anything?

KAT: What?

GWEN: You're only defending him 'cause he's your mate.

KAT: Why the fuck do you need us to tell you not to rape people?

JEREMY: I'm defending him because he didn't do anything.

BENNY: Kat, let's cool it on the R-word.

KAT: No. I'm being honest.

GWEN: Sure.

BENNY: Why are you being so Catholic about this?

JEREMY: [*to* GWEN] He's your mate too, by the way.

LUKE: I drove you to school for weeks when your car broke down.

KAT: What's your point?

LUKE: I fucking drove you here.

KAT: What's your point?

LUKE: Why would you get in the car with me if you thought I was a rapist, why wouldn't you say something?

NICOLE: Well, I mean they were just rumours.

LUKE: [*to* KAT] But you believe them?

KAT: I believe women.

LUKE: But not me?

KAT: No, not you.

LUKE: … The guy you've known since you were eleven.

GWEN: That's not what this is about.

KAT: That's exactly why I don't believe you.

GWEN: We can't just ignore things you do because you are our friend.

WILLA: No Gwen, he didn't do anything, and we know that because we know him.

KAT: Why are you defending him? He's a creep to you all the time.

WILLA: No, he's not.

KAT: He's always talking about how he's fucking you—

LUKE: That's a joke.

KAT: —and feeling you up—

LUKE: That's a fucking joke.

KAT: It isn't funny.

LUKE: But jokes about the Holocaust are fair game?

GWEN: It's the constant jokes though, Luke.

LUKE: I'm just … Tell them, Willa!

WILLA: Yeah, he's just playing.

TILLY: Yeah, like every single thing that comes out of his mouth is sexist.

KAT: You are brainwashed.

WILLA: No. I'm not.

JEREMY: So, what, now if someone tells a joke they're automatically guilty of rape?

KAT: You've said it makes you uncomfortable.

TILLY: [*to* JEREMY] It's rape culture.

LUKE: What is she talking about?

WILLA: It's fine.

JEREMY: What does that even mean?

LUKE: No, what is she talking about?

GWEN: His jokes normalise sexual violence.

NICOLE: So, every other girl is a liar then I guess, Willa?

JEREMY: No, they don't.

GWEN: Yes.

LUKE: If you felt uncomfortable why didn't you say anything?

GWEN: Yes, they do.

WILLA: I didn't feel uncomfortable.

KAT: But I mean you did.

LUKE: I feel like I am on fucking trial here!

GWEN: Benny?

BENNY: What?

GWEN: You haven't said anything.

BENNY: Oh, I am Switzerland.

TILLY: There is no rape in Switzerland.

BENNY: No, I am Switzerland about Luke.

LUKE: Thanks dude, real fucking endorsement.

GWEN: You're not allowed to be Switzerland about this.

BENNY: If Switzerland could be Switzerland in THE HOLOCAUST. I'm pretty sure I can be Switzerland about this.

KAT: Well, clearly not 'cause you were the one who said his name.

BENNY: I just want to put it out there, I'd fuck you, Luke.

KAT: Cool?

BENNY: And if you came on to me it'd be a yes.

TILLY: Dude.

BENNY: Alcohol no alcohol.

WILLA: Can't you see he's upset!

LUKE: I just … can't believe you all think this about me.

Silence.

I mean, you're my friends. Like how?

KAT: Just admit it.

TILLY: You can't lie.

LUKE: I'm not fucking lying.

KAT: Don't play dumb.

BENNY: Luke, we saw it.

LUKE: Saw what?

NICOLE: Why are you lying about this?

KAT: Why are you fucking upset, you aren't the one who was raped?

LUKE: I didn't rape anyone! Jeremy?

JEREMY: Dude, I don't know.

LUKE: What do you mean you don't know?

JEREMY: I'm just saying, maybe you didn't realise what you were doing.

KAT: Admit what you did, Luke.

LUKE: I didn't do anything.

NICOLE: Just say it

LUKE: I didn't do it.

GWEN: The more you deny it, the more guilty you look.

LUKE: This is crazy.

KAT: Say it, Luke.

LUKE: No.

JEREMY: Dude, maybe.

LUKE: No, I won't say it. I didn't fucking rape someone!

KAT *grabs a pen.*

KAT: You aren't playing the game properly. So, I'm going to have to cross your name out.

WILLA: Kat, no! Don't fuck with the book.

NICOLE: Do it, he's a fucking creep.

GWEN: Luke just admit it and we can move on.

TILLY: Lying about it is worse dude.

KAT: Fuck this.

KAT *opens the book.* LUKE *is distraught.*

LUKE: Okay I did it!

WILLA: Luke.

LUKE: Don't cross out my name.

KAT: Okay.

Pause.

NICOLE: See, it wasn't that hard.

LUKE, *visibly upset, gets up and slowly walks to the door. Everyone watches him. He stops in front of it.*

LUKE: I'm leaving.

WILLA: I think you should stay.

LUKE: No, I want to go home.

He stares at the door, not moving. His muscles are tense, there is a clear physical indication that he is trying to leave with no success.

[*Screaming*] I want to go home!

JEREMY: You should probably just stay here until the morning.

LUKE: I don't want to be in this house with that fucking book anymore.

GWEN: Luke, stay. At least until the morning.

LUKE: You know what. Fuck it.

WILLA: Luke, you need to calm down a bit.

LUKE: No, this is a party, right?

KAT: Right.

LUKE: What I need to do is fucking dance.

LUKE *turns on the record player.*

Woo!

BENNY: What is happening?

LUKE: We're dancing. It's a party. So, let's dance. Come on!

> WILLA *gets up and dances with him*

KAT: Willa what are you doing?

WILLA: I'm not going to let him dance alone, that's sad.

NICOLE: This is so crazy.

LUKE: Yes, thank you Nicole, we are just having some fun.

TILLY: You guys are weird.

LUKE: Gwen, you wanted a party, show us your moves then?

BENNY: Look at this move I learnt from a dancing TikTok boy.

GWEN: I—

LUKE: Don't say no, just dance.

KAT: [*to* BENNY] Keep going, don't stop.

GWEN: I don't really dance.

LUKE: And there lies your problem!

> TILLY *gets up and begins to dance.*

JEREMY: Okay we're up.

GWEN: Jeremy.

LUKE: Willa let's show them our move.

WILLA: Oh my God! Yes.

> LUKE *and* WILLA *do some sort of swing move, or a couple's dance move.*

NICOLE: When did you guys learn that?

WILLA: We have a whole routine.

> *Everyone is dancing (except* GWEN*).* WILLA *is teaching* NICOLE *how to do the swing move,* KAT *and* BENNY *are ironically doing TikTok dances,* JEREMY *and* TILLY *are dancing together.* GWEN *stops the music.*

LUKE: Bro.

GWEN: That's enough.

KAT: Yeah, we wouldn't want to have too much fun at a party.

GWEN: You can't just dance after everything that's happened.

TILLY: We did.

GWEN: No. Enough. We need to take this seriously.

KAT: What seriously?

GWEN: You haven't tried to leave.

NICOLE: Yes, I have when I first got here.

GWEN: But that wasn't—just can you try to leave please?

NICOLE: No, I don't want to leave.

GWEN: Leave, Nicole!

> NICOLE *walks toward the door but stops.*

NICOLE: No, I don't want to leave.

GWEN: Oh, come on!

WILLA: Guys what if we are dead?

JEREMY: Please don't start this again.

WILLA: No, I'm serious.

BENNY: What if Willa didn't hit a possum, and we were actually in a really big car crash?

NICOLE: Half of us weren't in the car.

BENNY: Yeah, but maybe you are being visited by us right now.

GWEN: But we can touch you?

WILLA: Tactile hallucination.

NICOLE: Okay, not that I'm feeding into this but if you think you are dead, we should cover the mirrors.

GWEN: What?

KAT: I keep thinking I see people in them, like people other than me.

NICOLE: It's the lights. When there isn't much light, your brain can't recognise your own face and it thinks it's seeing someone else.

WILLA: That's crazy.

NICOLE: But we should cover them.

BENNY: Why?

NICOLE: I read on Reddit that like funeral homes, and like places where people are mourning, cover the mirrors so that the spirits don't see themselves.

KAT: What happens if they see themselves in the mirror?

NICOLE: They get stuck in there, in the house.

BENNY: I've looked in the mirror like six times.

NICOLE: That's not the only reason, in like kabbalah—

TILLY: That's like Jewish celebrity one, right?

NICOLE: Yeah, they think that like evil spirits come and find you when you are vulnerable using mirrors.

GWEN: Why did we even bring the mirrors down?

WILLA: For protection!

LUKE: It was before we thought we might be dead.

TILLY: We're not dead, we're just stuck.

JEREMY: What?

TILLY: Playing the game.

JEREMY: We can stop.

TILLY: Who hasn't gone yet?

LUKE: Are we seriously going to keep playing?

Pause. The lights flicker.

TILLY: I don't think it's a good idea to stop in the middle.

NICOLE: Yeah.

WILLA: Especially with the book.

JEREMY: We can just rip the page out of the book.

LUKE: No, no, no, don't do that.

JEREMY: Why not?

LUKE: I shouldn't have written in that book in the fucking first place please don't make it worse.

NICOLE: Who hasn't gone?

JEREMY: We aren't seriously going to keep playing.

NICOLE: Let's just say hypothetically 'something' is going on here. I don't want to do anything that could make it worse.

WILLA: Have you read all the fucked up stories about Ouija boards, like when people stop the wrong way?

GWEN: This isn't a Ouija board.

Pause.

TILLY: Maybe it's Dad.

GWEN: What?

TILLY: He would want us to keep playing the game.

GWEN: Don't be ridiculous.

TILLY: I'm not.

GWEN: You're being disrespectful.

TILLY: Would it be so bad? If he was here?

WILLA: Maybe he's here, Tilly.

GWEN: Don't encourage her.

TILLY: I want him to be here.

GWEN: Well, he's not.

JEREMY: Gwen.

GWEN: He's not and she needs to get over it.

Pause.

WILLA: I have a question!

WILLA *whispers a question in* LUKE*'s ear.*

LUKE: Benny.

BENNY: Fuck.

The coin is flipped, it lands on heads.

Luke, don't.

LUKE: What did you ask me?

WILLA: Who is the most likely to fuck Kat.

NICOLE: HA!

LUKE: I'm not joking.

TILLY: Yeah yeah.

GWEN: Why would you even ask that?

WILLA: She called me a slut and him a rapist. I was wondering if there was anyone brave enough to still want to sleep with her. It's a joke.

LUKE: My answer wasn't a joke. He talks about her all the time.

GWEN: Yeah, they are best friends.

JEREMY: No, not like that.

GWEN: What?

JEREMY: Locker room talk.

LUKE: Bet you wish you weren't Switzerland now. Made it pretty clear you aren't my mate, hey?

BENNY: Luke I was just—

LUKE: He talks about how he thinks about you guys getting drunk and hooking up. And what parts of you he wants to grab.

KAT: That's enough. I don't believe you at all.

LUKE: The game doesn't work unless we tell the truth.

KAT: Then come up with a more believable truth.

LUKE: He talks about your tits and how you undress around him.

KAT: Okay Benny, that's gross you shouldn't do that. That's like a privacy thing.

JEREMY: He wants you.

KAT: Nah, he's trying to make you guys laugh.

BENNY: I want you.

KAT: What?

> *Pause.*

BENNY: I want you.

KAT: No, you don't, you're gay.

> BENNY *does not get aggressive or dramatic. This is the most serious and real that he has ever been.*

BENNY: I do. I think about you all the time.

KAT: Um. Okay. Um. You're confused.

BENNY: Yeah, I'm confused.

GWEN: Maybe it's just because you two hang out so much?

TILLY: Yeah, maybe you are just lonely.

BENNY: I'm not lonely—can you just … Kat.

KAT: You are gay. Like gay gay. Like 'came out to me at eleven' gay.

BENNY: I know.

KAT: Exactly! So, you just think you like me, but you are just projecting or something.

BENNY: I'm not projecting. I want you.

KAT: I don't—okay haha very funny, guys.

BENNY: What's funny?

KAT: I'm not stupid this is obviously a prank.

BENNY: No.

KAT: You can give it up, Benjamin.

BENNY: No, I'm not joking.

KAT: Yes, you are.

BENNY: Why would I do that?

KAT: Exactly why the fuck would you say that you like me like that unless you were trying to, I don't know, teach me a lesson.

BENNY: Because I do. Why are you acting like this?

KAT: Because you are so obviously lying to me.

BENNY: I'm not lying. I don't get to choose how I feel. I like you. I can't do anything about that. Why are there rules for me? For how I'm allowed to feel?

WILLA: There aren't.

BENNY: Yes! There are. I can't even be honest about how I'm feeling without it being a thing.

NICOLE: It's not a thing.

BENNY: It is! Don't tell me that it isn't while you stand there telling me that who I like is confusing.

GWEN: No, I was just saying from my perspective, which is that of a cis, white, heterosexual-presenting woman, so you know—limited, I can see why it would be confusing for Kat.

BENNY: For Kat? I'm gay so I'm obviously lying about having feelings for her right? Unless I'm not in which case I'm lying about being gay right? But I'm not lying. About anything!

GWEN: Well, you can't be both.

BENNY: Why do you—How is that fair?

NICOLE: No-one said it was fair, it's just being gay means something—specific.

BENNY: So, I'm not gay?

NICOLE: No.

BENNY: So, I'm lying?

WILLA: We aren't saying that.

BENNY: Just that I'm confused?

NICOLE: No just that words have meanings …

BENNY: That I don't know my own feelings?

NICOLE: … like we can't just change things to suit.

BENNY: How is it a thing? That just like having a feeling will change how everyone sees me?

GWEN: No, you're allowed to have your feelings.

BENNY: Kat.

GWEN: There's just like …

BENNY: I feel guilty for liking you, Kat. I feel like a fraud. I feel like I have to pretend I don't.

> KAT *looks at* BENNY *searching for the words. She tries to speak a few times before taking a step back.*

KAT: You can't just like me. That's not how it works.

> *Pause.*

BENNY: Fuck this, I'm leaving.

He starts walking toward the door.

TILLY: No, no, no, no, no, no, no.

> *He stops in his tracks. Without actually moving another attempt is made to get closer to the door.*

BENNY: FUCK!

KAT: Oh my God, stop being so dramatic.

WILLA: We have to keep playing right?

LUKE: For how long? For the rest of time?

BENNY: I want to leave.

JEREMY: We all want to leave, dude.

TILLY: We have to play until we've all told the truth.

JEREMY: Why?

WILLA: Jeremy, come on. I get that you don't want to believe and shit. But we did something when we put our names in that book.

NICOLE: We shouldn't have messed with it. But we did and now …

JEREMY: Now what, we have to lose our fucking minds?

WILLA: No, we just can't—we have to be careful. I don't want my life to be ruined 'cause I played some game.

LUKE: Yeah neither.

JEREMY: Are you serious?

TILLY: Jer. You need to just trust us.

LUKE: Well, who the fuck is still hiding shit?

BENNY: What?

LUKE: That's how we get this done isn't it? Get it all out?

GWEN: Are you just making shit up?

TILLY: No, that's what we decided.

WILLA: What do you mean?

TILLY: Paranoia is fuelled by the unknown. So, we just need to get rid of the unknown.

NICOLE: I read online that things like this usually stop when the sun comes up. Like that you can just wait it out.

KAT: That's reassuring.

WILLA: I don't think we should leave until the sun comes up.

LUKE: Nah, let's start asking questions.

TILLY: Can we ask a question if we know the answer?

JEREMY: I mean you are making it all up, so why not?

TILLY: Okay well I have a question.

> TILLY *whispers in* GWEN*'s ear.*

GWEN: Kat.

> *The coin is flipped it lands on tails. They all stare.*

JEREMY: Tails.

BENNY: Wait what does that mean?

WILLA: It means we don't get to find out.

LUKE: But it's a broken coin, it only lands on heads.

KAT: Clearly not, three-head.

TILLY: Fuck that.

> *She grabs the coin and flips it again.*

WILLA: No Tilly!

TILLY: Heads.

LUKE: That's better.

WILLA: You can't do that.

TILLY: Ask the question, Gwen.

KAT: Go on.

GWEN: Who's the meanest person here?

KAT: 'Cause of what I just did? I mean, you all agree with me, right?

GWEN: That's not why I said you.

KAT: Alright, I get that I'm honest and that pisses you all off but—

GWEN: Not that either.

KAT: Okay—what did I do?

GWEN: Think about it.

LUKE: Oh shit, I know what she's talking about.

> LUKE *whispers in* JEREMY*'s ear.*

JEREMY: Gwen, don't.

GWEN: Don't what?

BENNY: It's the rules.

JEREMY: Collateral damage.

WILLA: Wait, Luke, tell me.

LUKE: Nah nah.

GWEN: Come on, Kat.

KAT: Like I barely care enough about anything for it to be worth lying so I don't know.

GWEN: Let's just get it all out.

KAT: I honestly have no idea what you are talking about.

TILLY: Gwen.

GWEN: You're so funny, Kat.

KAT: Um thank you?

GWEN: You just love a good joke.

KAT: Sure, weirdo.

GWEN: What's the worst thing you've ever done to get a laugh?

BENNY: Oh shit.

KAT: I—

GWEN: You have to explain, that's part of the game.

LUKE: Can we just, there … tails, moving on …

GWEN: No.

JEREMY: Gwen, what are you doing?

WILLA: Wait, what is it?

GWEN: Oh, so now you don't like the attention?

WILLA: Can someone just explain?

GWEN: Say it or I will.

KAT: You won't.

GWEN: Kat became friends with you as a joke.

LUKE: Jesus fuck.

WILLA: What?

NICOLE: Willa.

WILLA: Me?

GWEN: Yes.

WILLA: Just me?

GWEN: Yes.

WILLA: But why?

KAT: You're just very different to me.

WILLA: What does that mean?

GWEN: It's a nice way of calling you a bimbo.

WILLA: And you all knew?

LUKE: I wasn't in on it I just knew about it promise.

WILLA: But you didn't tell me.

LUKE: Willa—

WILLA: Don't.

Silence.

Why would you do that?

KAT: I'm your friend Willa, let's just drop it.

WILLA: You wanted to make me look like an idiot.

KAT: No.

WILLA: You made me look like an idiot.

JEREMY: None of us think that you're an idiot.

KAT *laughs.*

WILLA: Everyone warned me about you. They told me what an absolute fucking bitch you were.

KAT: Okay Willa, knock yourself out.

WILLA: So, I guess I *am* an idiot for not listening.

KAT: Maybe.

WILLA: When I walk out that door, that will be the last time you will ever see me.

Pause.

KAT: Boo-fucking-hoo.

NICOLE: Oh my God.

WILLA: There we go.

KAT: I don't need you.

WILLA: There's the Kat I know.

KAT: People come, and people go, Willa.

WILLA: Couldn't risk a vulnerable moment.

KAT: If you need me to be the bad person in your story, happy to do that for you.

GWEN: Kaaaat.

KAT: But I'm not going to feel bad about what I did, it was funny.

TILLY: Come on.

KAT: You are all acting like I'm some evil person but it's crazy how I know all of your secrets. You all trusted me, because you know I'm honest.

GWEN: No, you are a bitch, that has nothing to do with being honest.

KAT: Gwen, if you want to see a bitch—

GWEN: Kat, I can dish just as hard as you, so I'd be careful.

KAT: I'm not so sure about that.

GWEN: You think you've got dirt on me?

KAT: I know I've got dirt on you.

Pause.

I don't want to say it.

GWEN: Say it or we will never fucking get out of here.

KAT: Fine. Nicole, come here. The answer is Gwen, okay?

KAT *whispers in* NICOLE*'s ear.* NICOLE*'s face drops.*

NICOLE: Gwen.

The coin is flipped, it lands on heads.

KAT: Tell them the question.

NICOLE: Who killed Mr Michaels?

TILLY: What?

KAT: What's the last thing you said to your dad, Gwen?

TILLY: What's she talking about?

KAT: Come on, Gwen, play the game.

GWEN: I said that I wished he was dead.

TILLY: Gwen are you fucking serious?

GWEN: Yes.

Silence.

TILLY *runs out of the room.*

WILLA: It's not your fault.

GWEN: Maybe not.

NICOLE: No, he was …

GWEN: [*contained but repressed*] Maybe it was what I said though. Or something I said or didn't say the day before or the day before that.

LUKE: Nah, you shouldn't blame yourself.

GWEN: It's fine. There are a thousand different choices I could have made over a thousand different days. There's nothing I can do about that. I didn't know—

WILLA: Exactly.

GWEN: And even if I did know, even if I knew which choice mattered, I wouldn't know how to make the right choice.

BENNY: You couldn't.

GWEN: And I mean he's dead! It's done! I can't—there are one thousand

different choices I can't make now. There are so many choices
I can't make.

Pause.

And I try to work it out, to think things through, but it's like ...
People die! And then there's no time! No choice. No way to fix it.
And so, he is gone.

WILLA: Yeah. I'm sorry.

They stand in silence for a moment.

GWEN: Can we just—Can we get out of this room for a second?

BENNY: Want to go upstairs maybe?

JEREMY: Yeah, let's go upstairs, change of scenery.

GWEN: Yeah.

LUKE: Okay, come on. I don't think I've ever been in your room, Gwen.

JEREMY: We can check on Tilly too.

The group starts to go upstairs but KAT *lingers.*

BENNY: Are you coming?

KAT: I don't know I feel like I should stay?

BENNY: It was a kind of fucked-up thing to do ...

KAT: No, that's not what I mean. Forget about it, let's go.

They go upstairs. TILLY *enters the room silently. She is visibly
upset. She approaches the book and sits with it. She gently
touches the book. She sniffles trying to gather herself, placing
her hand firmly on the book.*

TILLY: Dad?

Dad are you here?

The lights flicker. She stands up.

[*Scared*] Daddy?

*She turns around looking for him in the room. She pivots back
thinking she might have seen something in the mirrors.*

She didn't mean it.

*She stares deeply into the mirror for a moment. It is unclear if
she is looking at herself or behind.* TILLY *breathes in sharply,*

sure that she's seen something in the mirror. She touches her own hand in the mirror.

I want to leave the party.

She looks around the room but hears footsteps coming from upstairs. She quickly exits to the bathroom.

GWEN: She'll come down when she wants to.

JEREMY: Should one of us check on her?

BENNY: She's probably getting high.

GWEN: Hey!

WILLA: To be honest, I was thinking the same thing.

GWEN: She wants attention, she'll come back when she's not getting it.

JEREMY: Gwen, be nice.

GWEN: It's true.

NICOLE: Well, we kind of need her, that's all.

LUKE: Why?

NICOLE: Because we need her to come clean about something.

LUKE: Oh, is she the last one?

BENNY: No, she's not.

WILLA: Who else?

BENNY: Nicole.

NICOLE: No, I—when I got here Gwen and I talked it out.

BENNY: That wasn't in the game.

NICOLE: Well, I don't have anything I need to be honest about other than that.

BENNY: Cap.

JEREMY: What do you mean?

WILLA: Come on, no bully.

BENNY: My cousin goes to your school, Nic.

NICOLE: Okay cool.

BENNY: She told me some crazy stuff about you.

NICOLE: I don't know what you're talking about.

WILLA: Oh my God, what are you doing at your new school?

NICOLE: Nothing.

GWEN: No, come on, tell us.

LUKE: Seem pretty cagey there, Nic.

WILLA: Are you in like a gang?

KAT: Willa what are you talking about?

WILLA: I never go to that side of town. I don't know.

JEREMY: Stop wasting time and ask a question.

BENNY *whispers in* GWEN*'s ear.*

GWEN: Nicole.

BENNY: Flip the coin.

The coin is flipped, it lands on heads.

GWEN: Who is the best storyteller?

WILLA: Duh, Nic has always been a writer.

KAT: That's so fucking boring.

BENNY: Told any good stories lately, Nicole?

KAT: Like what a waste of a build-up.

NICOLE: I literally don't know what you are talking about.

BENNY: You are going to make me tell them?

WILLA: Ooooo.

NICOLE: Tell them what?

BENNY: The little story you've been telling at your new school.

NICOLE: I don't know what you've heard but it's probably wrong.

BENNY: You know what would be messed up Nicole? If when you got to your new school, you told everyone that your dad killed himself.

GWEN: What's he talking about?

LUKE: What? That's—

BENNY: But no, that wouldn't be enough for you, would it? You'd also want to tell everyone your mum was dying of cancer.

JEREMY *looks up.*

NICOLE: No, it's—

BENNY: 'Cause we all know your parents are fine.

KAT: No way.

BENNY: That didn't happen to you, did it? It happened to Gwen and to Tilly and to Jeremy.

WILLA: Nicole, you didn't.

BENNY: Nothing makes you a celebrity like being a victim. Easy way to get popular, hey?

NICOLE: It wasn't about that, I was—

GWEN: You have to be kidding.

BENNY: I heard you showed around the booklet from the funeral service, but you were in it? I wonder how you made that happen?

LUKE: Wha—Why?

WILLA: [*whispering*] That is so fucked up.

GWEN: Nicole, that better not be true.

BENNY: Pretty psycho, hey? But I mean it's a great story, people love a story when they think it's real.

NICOLE: I can explain.

KAT: Nicole, that's pathological.

BENNY: That's not the half of it.

NICOLE: Wait.

BENNY: Imagine how much of a psycho you'd have to be to take photos of your friend's mum in a hospital bed and pretend they were yours.

JEREMY: Hang on.

BENNY: Gotta be able to back up your story.

JEREMY: My mum? You've been using pictures of my mum??

NICOLE: [*unconvincingly*] I don't know what he's talking about.

WILLA: Nic, you can't lie.

GWEN: No seems like she can't help it.

JEREMY: My mum?

LUKE: Bro, calm down.

NICOLE: He's lying. I didn't—

> JEREMY *throws the book toward* NICOLE.

JEREMY: TELL THE FUCKING TRUTH.

NICOLE: He broke the book.

WILLA: Oh my God, we are so fucked.

BENNY: It's fine, the game is done.

GWEN: [*to* JEREMY] Look at me babe.

KAT: No, it's not, there's still Tilly.

NICOLE: Gwen.

GWEN: No. You don't SPEAK to us anymore.

WILLA: You can't throw the book, that's not okay.

BENNY: Maybe we can fix it?

KAT: It's fucked, guys.

GWEN: Jeremy?

LUKE: If we don't fix that book, I—

BENNY: Well, we have to try.

LUKE: —I will become a full-blown Catholic like right now.

GWEN: Just breathe.

LUKE: Like I will go into that bathroom and baptise myself, I don't care.

WILLA: [*to* GWEN] Is he okay?

LUKE: I am not staying in some house with spirits and shit / and just testing my luck.

GWEN: There aren't spirits.

JEREMY: I want Tilly.

GWEN: Tilly?

> *Everyone looks at* JEREMY, *interested.* GWEN *waits for a response.*

Why would you want Tilly?

LUKE: Where even is Tilly?

GWEN: Why would you want my sister, Jeremy?

> JEREMY *stands up and walks away from* GWEN *pressing his eyes into his hands. Everyone is silent. He turns to face* GWEN.

JEREMY: Because I'm in love with her.

> *Everyone is shocked.* GWEN *is stunned.*

GWEN: Okay.

What do you mean by that?

JEREMY: I never wanted to hurt you.

GWEN: How have you hurt me, Jeremy?

JEREMY: I'm sorry.

GWEN: You have to say it.

> JEREMY *says nothing.*

You have to tell me the truth.

JEREMY: I'm sorry.

GWEN: How long?

JEREMY: A few months.

GWEN: That makes sense.

WILLA: [*whispering to* NICOLE] Where's Tilly?

GWEN: And did they know?

NICOLE: I don't know.

She looks at all the other friends standing around the room.

JEREMY: No.

I'm sorry.

GWEN: How long have you been sorry?

JEREMY: I—

GWEN: Just today? Or the whole time?

Pause. JEREMY *doesn't reply.*

I'm perfect.

LUKE *snorts.*

BENNY: Shh.

GWEN: Right, Jeremy? That's the truth, isn't it? I'm pretty and I'm smart and I'm funny and thoughtful and I'm not needy.

JEREMY: I know.

GWEN: I do everything right. And I guess now I get why it always felt like I was doing something wrong, like it was upsetting you. Because you didn't want it from me, right?

JEREMY: There's just a lot going on right now.

GWEN: I have been trying to be there for you.

JEREMY: I know.

KAT: Should we leave?

BENNY: We can't leave, remember.

JEREMY: I didn't mean to—

GWEN: It's okay.

Pause.

I'm ready to forgive you.

JEREMY: What?

GWEN: I'm ready to forgive you. You told me the truth. You didn't try to lie to me. I didn't find out by myself. And now it's out there and it's not hanging over us. So, we don't have to take it forward with us.

JEREMY: Gwen.

GWEN: Right? Right? We can do that. It's not a big deal.

JEREMY: I don't want to be with you.

GWEN: Yes, you do.

LUKE: Offt.

NICOLE: Shut up.

JEREMY: No.

GWEN: No, yes, you do.

JEREMY: I want to be / with—

GWEN: You're not / allowed to be with her.

JEREMY: Tilly.

GWEN: No.

JEREMY: Gwen, that's what I want.

GWEN: You're not allowed to do that.

KAT: She's kind of not here anyway.

NICOLE: Kat.

GWEN: Why?

JEREMY: She needs me.

GWEN: I need you.

JEREMY: No, you don't.

GWEN: That's so fucked up Jeremy.

JEREMY: I'm sorry.

GWEN: What? You just want her 'cause she's broken? How fucked up
    is that?

JEREMY: No.

GWEN: You think you're going to fix her; you think you're going to
    make her better?

JEREMY: I can try.

GWEN: You think you are the only person to try?

JEREMY: No, I didn't mean it / like—

GWEN: She's a selfish little brat who loves being damaged.

KAT: Said with love, of course.

GWEN: Kat, shut the fuck up.

LUKE: Sheesh.

GWEN: I gave her everything. I protected her. She didn't go through it
    like I did. She doesn't get to be broken and you don't get to love
    her for it.

JEREMY: Gwen—

GWEN: No. I forgave you. You made a fucking mess and I cleaned it up.

JEREMY: I—

GWEN: I did my part now you do yours.

WILLA: [*whispering*] I need to pee.

BENNY: [*whispering*] What?

WILLA: [*slightly louder*] I need to pee.

BENNY: [*whispering*] Then go.

JEREMY: This is not, oh my God, Gwen, you don't get to control this.

WILLA: But the toilet's over there.

BENNY: Just go.

JEREMY: I can't like choose how I—

> WILLA *tip toes across the room through the middle of the argument.*

WILLA: Sorry! Sorry! Sorry!

GWEN: Actually, yes you fucking can.

LUKE: Cool, so she's lost it.

GWEN: Get the fuck out of my house.

LUKE: I have literally been trying to do that like all night.

JEREMY: It's just different.

GWEN: Yes, but how, Jeremy?

JEREMY: It's just—

LUKE: Different.

GWEN: Shut. Up.

JEREMY: She doesn't try to fix it.

> *Silence.*

GWEN: I am sorry for trying to help.

JEREMY: You can't help.

GWEN: That's not true though.

JEREMY: You see, Gwen?

GWEN: No, I'm not talking about your mum.

> WILLA *stands at the doorway.*

WILLA: Guys.

JEREMY: But it is about my mum. It's that simple.

GWEN: No, it's actually not and you have to trust me on this because I know and I'm trying to help you.

WILLA: Hey guys.

JEREMY: You don't know and it's not helping.

GWEN: When she goes—

JEREMY: Stop.

BENNY: Will, you can cross the room it's fine.

GWEN: You aren't going to be prepared. You will think you are ready, but you won't be.

JEREMY: I'll be fine.

GWEN: No, you don't know how you are going to react when it happens. How your body is going to react.

WILLA: I think Tilly's dead.

Pause.

JEREMY *and* LUKE *run to the bathroom.*

BENNY: What do you mean you think?!

NICOLE: Gwen.

WILLA: I—

WILLA *sobs.*

NICOLE: Gwen.

KAT: Willa, come here.

GWEN: [*existential*] What?!

NICOLE: Look at me.

GWEN: WHAT!?

LUKE *and* JEREMY *carry* TILLY *into the room.*

JEREMY: She's not dead, she's not dead.

LUKE: She must have taken some shit.

NICOLE: What shit?

LUKE: I don't know isn't that what she does?

GWEN *stands staring at* TILLY *on the ground.*

JEREMY: Tilly, Tilly, open your eyes.

LUKE: Gwen, what do we do?

JEREMY: Tilly!

LUKE: Should we do CPR?

KAT: We should call someone.

WILLA: I just walked in, and she was like lying there and I thought she just like passed out but then I looked again and …

LUKE: She's not dead.

BENNY: It's okay, it's okay, it's going to be okay.

GWEN *walks away and sits on the floor. Everyone begins to unravel except for* KAT *who pushes to fix things.*

KAT: [*to* GWEN] What are you doing? Whatareyoudoing whatareyoudoing? Get up!

NICOLE: Check her airway. Tilly?

KAT: Gwen, where did you put our phones. Gwen? GWEN.

WILLA: We can't use the phones, that's how they get us.

KAT: I can't see anything with these fucking lights. Google turn the lights up.

LUKE: Put her on her side.

KAT: Willa, where did Gwen put the phones?

WILLA: I—I don't know.

WILLA *is wailing,* GWEN *is silent facing away from* TILLY.

KAT: I can't see. GOD. Google, turn up the lights!

JEREMY: Get the book.

LUKE: What?

JEREMY: Get the book!

KAT: Hey Google, call the ambulance.

GOOGLE: I am sorry that feature has not been activated.

KAT *screams.*

LUKE: I don't know what to do, what do we do? Gwen?

NICOLE: I'm going to look for the phones.

NICOLE *does not move.*

KAT: Willa stop crying and go and get an adult.

WILLA: We can't go outside.

KAT: We can go outside, we are being ridiculous.

WILLA: I don't want to go outside.

KAT: Tilly is going to die, Willa.

WILLA: No, we have to wait.

KAT: Did you hear me?!

WILLA: Those are the rules!

LUKE: She's getting like really cold. Gwen? She's getting cold.

KAT *crouches in front of* GWEN.

KAT: Gwen you have to snap out of it. I need you to tell me where you put our phones. Tilly needs you.

NICOLE: I'll grab the blankets.

KAT: Yes, cover her!

JEREMY: No cover the mirrors!

KAT: What!?

JEREMY: She'll get stuck in here; we have to cover the mirrors.

KAT: Benny, you have to go.

> BENNY *shakes his head.* JEREMY *tries to fix the broken book.*

JEREMY: We have to fix it.

LUKE: We can't, dude.

JEREMY: I broke it. I'm sorry Til, I broke it.

KAT: You have to go, Nicole. Now.

NICOLE: I'm not walking out of here again.

KAT: Are you—Someone has to go!

NICOLE: I'm sorry, I can't.

KAT: Fine, I'll go then; this is fucking crazy.

> KAT *walks toward the door and opens it.*

WILLA: Kat!

> *She turns.*

The sun's almost up.

KAT: I—

WILLA: You could just wait. Like ten minutes.

> KAT *walks to the couch and sits down. The room slowly fills with light. No-one moves.*

THE END

CANBERRA YOUTH THEATRE PRESENTS

YOU CAN'T TELL ANYONE

BY JOANNA RICHARDS

WORLD PREMIERE
10–20 AUGUST 2023
THE COURTYARD STUDIO – CANBERRA THEATRE CENTRE

CAST

GWEN	ELLA BUCKLEY
TILLY	EMILY O'MAHONEY
JEREMY	JAKE ROBINSON
WILLA	JESSI GOODING
LUKE	ISAIAH PRICHARD
KAT	PARIS SCHARKIE
BENNY	LACHLAN HOUEN
NICOLE	BREANNA KELLY

CREATIVE TEAM

DIRECTOR	CAITLIN BAKER
SET & COSTUME DESIGNER	KATHLEEN KERSHAW
LIGHTING DESIGNER	ETHAN HAMILL
SOUND DESIGNER & COMPOSER	PATRICK HAESLER
STAGE MANAGER	RHILEY WINNETT

ACKNOWLEDGEMENTS

We greatly acknowledge the support of the ACT Government through artsACT, and Ainslie and Gorman Arts Centres. This production is supported by Canberra Theatre Centre, as part of a commitment to nurturing the young and emerging artists of the ACT.

You Can't Tell Anyone was the winner of Canberra Youth Theatre's 2021 Emerging Playwright Commission.

CANBERRA YOUTH THEATRE

THE VOICE OF YOUTH EXPRESSED THROUGH CHALLENGING AND INTELLIGENT THEATRE

Canberra Youth Theatre is one of the leading youth arts companies in Australia.

We develop opportunities for young people to collaborate, develop their artistic skills and create pathways to the professional arts sector.

We advocate for and amplify the voices of young people, providing a space for them to discover and express their creative selves.

We produce powerful theatre where young artists ignite urgent conversations, challenge the forces that shape them, and invite us to see the world from new perspectives.

Over our 50 year history, we have collaborated with thousands of young artists through productions, workshops, creative developments and community events. We have created works in our major theatres, public spaces, and national cultural institutions. We have toured around the country, and internationally.

Canberra Youth Theatre has grown and evolved significantly over the past five decades, constantly responding to the passions and perspectives of generations of young people, and adapting to changes in the way we create and experience live performance. We remain at the forefront of Australian youth theatre practice, creating innovative, accessible and challenging opportunities for young people to access and engage in professional-quality theatrical experiences.

From Debra Oswald's now Australian classic *Dags*, and works by writers Tommy Murphy, Mary Rachel Brown, Lachlan Philpott, Angela Betzien, Liv Hewson, Ross Mueller, Emily Sheehan, Jessica Bellamy, Cathy Petocz, Julian Larnach, and Tasnim Hossain, we have nurtured new voices and commissioned professional artists to create acclaimed works for young people.

We continue to nurture and develop young people, giving them a place to belong, to share their voice, and to inspire audiences of all ages.

Canberra Youth Theatre acknowledges the Ngunnawal and Ngambri peoples as the Traditional Owners of the lands on which we collaborate, share stories, and create art. We celebrate their rich history of over 60,000 years of culture and storytelling. We recognise their continuing connection to the lands and waters of our region. We pay our respects to their Elders past, present and emerging. Sovereignty was never ceded. Always was and always will be.

What was most important to me in writing this play was that it spoke the language of young adults. And so, while I wanted to explore complex topics and philosophical themes, for me it was necessary to stay true to the teenage tongue. We often underestimate the depth and complexity of teenagers' minds because of the way they speak about topics. However, the issues that play on the minds of young adults are the same ones that have haunted philosophers for years. In this play, although never stated explicitly, the ensemble grapple with philosophical problems such as: Plato's Cave, Aristotle's Good Life, Kant's Conception of Autonomy, Schopenhauer's Unconscious Repression, Nietzsche's Gay Science, Wittgenstein's Weltbild, Heidegger's Being, Arendt's Origins of Totalitarianism, Sartre's Existentialism, De Beauvoir's se faire objet, Freud's Hysteria, Jung's Paranoia, Derrida's Hauntology, Foucault's Discursive Sexualities, Baudrillard's Simulacra, Durkheim's Anomie, Debord's Spectacle, Lasch's Narcissism, and Fisher's Capitalist Realism. The questions of philosophy, which are also often central to art, are at their base human questions. Ideas that make up the fabric of our world before we even fully comprehend them.

While the language of the play is as realistic and naturalistic as possible, the action is surreal. Nothing feels quite right, and there is no stable reality for the characters or audience to grasp. I wanted to be able to explore the anomie of teenagers today, and what it is to exist in the transitory space between frameworks of understanding. The idea of social rules and contagion drives the work, and it is rooted in our deep human desire to believe in something and to be a part of the group. The subconscious adherence to a strong collective consciousness is something that I think is particularly relevant to youth today. The world is in a period of great uncertainty. Every day is tinged by the threat of natural disaster, disease, and war. Fact has given way to opinion. Dogged belief has outrun rationalism. Chaos looms just outside everyone's adherence to their own niche flimsy collective conscious. What once seemed like madness now seems sensible as we struggle to retain any sense of meaning, order, and belonging.

Why do we do nonsensical things? Even when they disadvantage us? Why do we stay at a party when we are having a terrible time? Why do we continue to associate with people who have hurt us deeply? These questions are more relevant today than ever. A culture of normlessness has produced a generational anomie; a melancholy caused by an inability to see where or how one fits into the world. It's melodramatic and surreal, and that's exactly what it feels like to be a teenager in the world today.

Joanna Richards

DIRECTOR'S NOTE

When you become an adult, it is very easy to become unkind to the teenager you used to be. You forget that the end of childhood can be a violent, messy affair — for you and for everyone else. In short, you overlook the realisation that no one gets out of growing up, alive.

I first encountered Joanna's play in the earliest stages of its development, and was struck by how familiar its characters seemed. They refused to be bogged down by the sometimes cloying optimism of 'young people' in theatre, but also refused to go anywhere near a cynical portrayal of lost youth. Instead, these characters — Gwen, Tilly, Jeremy, Benny, Kat, Luke, Willa, and Nicole — emerged as people torn up by the same desires we've been battling for aeons, all the while figuring out how to become their own north stars in a world that has turned off the lights, and in a house they have far outgrown.

This show brought me back to the versions of ourselves that we can't seem to get rid of as we move forward: the child inside us who cries out to be loved and to be known, even when it's no longer appropriate to say such things aloud. Our rehearsal room dived into that space where we begin to 'pretend' adulthood; where we learn to fear that we are secretly bad people, terrible friends, and somehow the only person learning how to do this for the first time — and getting it wrong. Now more than ever, we have rules and decisions thrust upon us, and are expected to get it all right the first time round. This play is about the child we were, the adult we're becoming, and desperately finding a way to make them meet in the middle.

As an early career artist, being trusted with this new work has been an incredibly affirming experience. To be trusted with a script, and a cast, and a whole wonderful production team is indescribable, and has been a joyous journey I will carry with me for the rest of my career. Canberra Youth Theatre has been there since the very beginning of me becoming an artist, and I am so grateful for their dedication for giving these stories to young people.

To work again with Patrick and Rhiley, and for the first time with Kathleen and Ethan, makes me so happy about the state of young creatives in our community. You readily took on my Pinterest boards and Spotify playlists, and I thank you for that. This cast is the best of what tomorrow brings for performance in Australia, and every rehearsal they have met my challenges with bravery and honesty. This is a hard script that doesn't cut corners, and they brought everything to every rehearsal.

Finally, a thank you to Joanna Richards and Luke Rogers. New work and new directors all in one go — that is what makes brave theatre, and makes me incredibly happy to work with, and know you both.

Caitlin Baker

CREATIVE TEAM

JOANNA RICHARDS | PLAYWRIGHT

Joanna is an actor and playwright based in Canberra. She has studied acting with the American Repertory Theatre Institute, The Moscow Art Theatre School, The Groundlings, and William Esper Studio. She studied writing for television at AFTRS, and sketch writing at The Second City. In 2020 she was selected for the Street Theatre's Early Phase Program. Joanna co-wrote the web series *Whirld* which was nominated for Best Series at the Sydney Web Fest and won Best Series at Paris Web Fest. In 2021, she started writing *Blonde Philosophy*, a sketch series for YouTube which uses character comedy to explore philosophical concepts. She is also a stand up and sketch comedian, performing at the Canberra Comedy Festival Gala, and at the PIT in NYC. Outside of the arts, Joanna works in the gender and diversity space as both a consultant and researcher, working for 50/50 by 2030 Foundation, Global Institute for Women's Leadership, the Office of Andrew Leigh, the Organisation for Security and Cooperation in Europe, the Australian Broadcasting Corporation, and the YWCA. In 2021, Joanna won Canberra Youth Theatre's Emerging Playwright Commission which led to the creation of *You Can't Tell Anyone*, her debut play.

CAITLIN BAKER | DIRECTOR

Caitlin Baker is a Canberra-based director, actor and theatre maker who is thrilled to be making her Canberra Youth Theatre directorial debut. Currently undertaking an English Honours Thesis which examines the use of violence as a dramatic dialect in the works of Sarah Kane, she was a Resident Artist with Canberra Youth Theatre in 2022, as well as holding a variety leadership positions across the ANU theatre community. Caitlin's previous directing credits include *macbitches* (2023), and *The Tempest* (2021), as well as assistant directing positions on *Collected Stories* (2022), *The Initiation* (2022), and *Soul Trading* (2022). Over the past few years, Caitlin has been seen moonlighting as an actor in various other shows, most recently including Canberra Youth Theatre's *How To Vote!* (2022), Alchemy Artistic's *The Boys* (2022), Canberra Repertory Society shows *Grapes of Wrath* (2020), *Brighton Beach Memoirs* (2020), and *The Governor's Family* (2021), the inaugural Emerge Company program's *Carpe DM* (2021), Law Revue's *Paddington 3* and the infamous 2019 ANU Shakespeare Society production of *Much Ado About Nothing*. As a terrible liar, and someone who wouldn't go back to being 18 even if you paid her, Caitlin hopes you enjoy *You Can't Tell Anyone* in all its complicated, honest and fantastic glory.

CREATIVE TEAM

KATHLEEN KERSHAW |
SET & COSTUME DESIGNER

Kathleen Kershaw is a set and costume designer working across Canberra and Sydney. Her practice features a deep engagement with story, character and research. She creates empathetic designs that hope to bring the action and audience together. In 2022 Kathleen created the Costume Design for NIDA's production of *Picnic at Hanging Rock*. She also wrote and directed a short film titled *Kelly* and was Production Designer for *The Job I Took* by Sophisticated Dingo, created as part of the Triple J Unearthed and NIDA Music Video Competition. For her graduating show, Kathleen designed the set and costumes for *Prem Patr*, presented first as a part of NIDA's 2022 Festival of Emerging Artists. Kathleen then travelled with *Prem Patr* to Jaipur, India for a season at Jawahar Kala Kendra. Kathleen is an engaged, energetic designer who is eager to continue making meaningful contributions to the shaping and telling of stories in live performance and film.

ETHAN HAMILL | LIGHTING DESIGNER

Ethan Hamill is an up-and-coming theatre practitioner, who specialises in Lighting and Video Design & Programming. Ethan has just finished his Bachelor of Fine Arts in Technical Theatre and Stage Management at the National Institute of Dramatic Art (NIDA). Ethan strives to keep up with new and emerging technology and is always trying to bring these technologies into theatre and live events. This has led him to have the opportunity to work on theatrical and dance shows, live concerts, events, and installations. Ethan's recent credits include Swing Lighting Operator on *Joseph and the Amazing Technicolour Dreamcoat* [Sydney Season] (2023), Lighting Designer for *The Magic Flute*, Lighting Designer for *The Trials*, Production Manager for *Falsettos* (2022), Lighting Designer for *Too Human* (2022), Lighting Designer *The Life That I Gave You* (2022), Co–Lighting Designer for *Scooby Doo and The Creepy Carnival* (2021), Co-Video Designer for *Eat Me* (STC/ NIDA Collaboration. Ethan is looking forward to being home after 3 years in Sydney, and getting to work again with the Canberra community, and with Canberra Youth Theatre, while expanding his career further in Sydney and surrounds.

PATRICK HAESLER | SOUND DESIGNER & COMPOSER

Patrick Haesler is a composer, performer, sound designer and recording artist from Canberra, Australia (Ngunnawal Country). Beginning as a trumpet player, Patrick has since branched into numerous musical fields, drawing influences from jazz and progressive music. In 2018 Patrick entered the world of theatre, acting as musical director for ANU's Arts Revue. Since then, he has reprised this role as well as composing music and designing sound for several theatre productions. These include *It's Not Creepy If They're Hot* (2019), *Macbeth* (2020), *The Tempest* (2021), *Dracula* (2022), *The Initiation* (2022), *How To Vote!* (2022), *Soul Trading* (2022) and *The Trials* (2023). Patrick has released soundtrack albums for many of these productions. Most recently, in July 2023 Patrick released the soundtrack for *How to Vote!*, a 23-track album featuring music from and inspired by the play. The album contains music in a range of styles to complement the play's blending of student drama and political thriller. Patrick's experience with a wide variety of musical genres, ensembles and production techniques have made him a versatile creative in the world of music and sound.

RHILEY WINNETT | STAGE MANAGER

Rhiley Winnett is a passionate, emerging stage manager, dedicated to working with young people and giving them the respect and opportunities that they may not be presented with otherwise. Rhiley has worked as stage manager on eight shows with Canberra Youth Theatre over the last few years including: *Normal* (2020), *Little Girls Alone in the Woods* (2021), *Two Twenty Somethings Decide Never To Be Stressed About Anything Ever Again. Ever.* (2021), *Dags* (2022), *The Initiation* (2022), *How to Vote!* (2022), *Soul Trading* (2022), and *The Trials* (2023). Rhiley was thrilled to be offered the opportunity to continue working with Canberra Youth Theatre as stage manager for their 2023 shows, and as part of their 2023 Resident Artist program.

CAST

ELLA BUCKLEY | GWEN

Ella Buckley is a passionate, local artist who has been an active member of Canberra's theatre scene for six years now, and has loved every minute of it. Ella is currently in her first year of a Bachelor of Arts/International Relations degree at ANU, and last year obtained her Certificate IV in Acting. Some of her favourite roles include Babe Botrelle in *Crimes of The Heart* (Canberra Repertory Society, 2023), Mon in *How To Vote!* (Canberra Youth Theatre, 2022) and Laurie Morton in *Brighton Beach Memoirs* (Canberra Rep, 2020). Creatively, Ella also enjoys writing and directing, and is currently working as a Workshop Artist with Canberra Youth Theatre.

JESSI GOODING | WILLA

Jessi Gooding has been involved with Canberra Youth Theatre for just over a year now, her highlights including Bronwyn in *Dags* (2022), and Alex in the 2022 Emerge Company's original production of *503: Service Unavailable*. She is currently studying arts at the ANU, and has enjoyed taking up ceramics and life drawing classes. She has always gravitated towards theatre as her ultimate safe space, and has been so lucky to meet such a broad community of talented artists along the way. Having been lucky enough to experience *You Can't Tell Anyone* at its earliest stages through creative developments, she has embraced the exciting journey of bringing this play to life and is absolutely thrilled for audiences to meet Willa.

LACHLAN HOUEN | BENNY

Lachlan Houen is currently studying Arts (English) at ANU on the lands of the Ngunnawal and Ngambri people, having moved here in 2021 from Wadawurrung land (Geelong). He is a passionate theatre maker, having been in many productions at ANU both in an acting (*Love and Information*, 2021; *When the Rain Stops Falling*, 2022) and production team capacity (Director: *The Laramie Project*, 2022; *An Ideal Husband*, 2022; *Mr Burns, A Post Electric Play*, 2023. Producer: *macbitches*, 2023; *Away*, 2023). He is extremely excited to be making his Canberra Youth Theatre production debut, and hopes to be involved in many more along the way.

BREANNA KELLY | NICOLE

Breanna Kelly is a passionate young actor and theatre maker who has been in the Canberra theatre scene for eight years now. They have performed many roles including Monica in *Dags* (Canberra Youth Theatre), Jo March in *Little Women*, Featured Dancer in *Be More Chill* (Budding Theatre), and they directed and performed as Linda in *Blood Brothers* (St Francis Xavier College). In 2021 they played the lead role of Emma in Hawker College's original radio musical *Multiverse Superstar*. Breanna also has the privilege this year to be part of Canberra Youth Theatre's Ambassadors Program.

EMILY O'MAHONEY | TILLY

Emily O'Mahoney is a Canberra-based actor and theatre-maker. Making her stage debut in 2020, she has performed in roles including Alina in *Little Girls Alone in the Woods* (Canberra Youth Theatre, 2021), Antigone in *The Burial at Thebes* (Merici College, 2022), and Jordan Baker in *The Great Gatsby* (Budding Entertainment, 2020). After getting a taste for theatre-making with her physical theatre piece *Exit Sign* for the ACTUP Youth Fringe (2022), Emily most recently performed with Canberra Youth Theatre's Emerge Company, showcasing their devised piece *Sympathetic Resonance* at the Uncharted Territory Festival. She has also recently co-founded Sunspot Cinematic, a local film production company focussed on developing and promoting the stories of young women.

ISAIAH PRICHARD | LUKE

Isaiah Prichard has been involved in theatre since he was five years old. Nearly 22 now, he is glad to have been involved in a few shows since his conception. Every performance has been such a delight. Even when Isaiah had to play the understudy for Nana in John X Presents' *Peter Pan and Wendy*. During this rehearsal process, he has enjoyed getting to know his character. He is even happier to be working under Caitlin Baker. Every day Isaiah tries his hardest to be happy. Longing for purpose.

CAST

JAKE ROBINSON | JEREMY

Jake Robinson started acting when he was 17 at The American School in Japan where he performed in plays and films, portraying a variety of characters. The two student films he was a part of both won awards at the Kanto Plain Film Festival for directing, acting, and sound design. One of his proudest productions was a student play about a father and mother who lost their daughter and how both their lives had deteriorated. Jake enjoys playing bass guitar, riding motorcycles, and playing a variety of games both online and in person.

PARIS SCHARKIE | KAT

Paris Scharkie is excited to be making her Canberra Youth Theatre debut in this show. Stepping outside of the comfort of student-led theatre productions for the first time, she hopes to immediately be scouted by a talent agent. Until that time occurs she will — and has — indulged herself in many student theatre productions at the ANU since starting her studies there in 2020. As an avid lover of Shakespeare, Paris made a start in ANU theatre as Sebastian in *Twelfth Night*, and has since gone on to perform in *Coriolanus*, *Chicago*, *Little Women*, *An Ideal Husband*, *The Lieutenant of Inishmore*, and *Bread Revue*. She has also directed for a Shakespeare showcase and is currently musical director for a production of *Mr Burns, A Post Electric Play*.

OUR PARTNERS

We gratefully acknowledge the generous support of our partners who are key to the success of our work.

GOVERNMENT PARTNER

Supported by

ACT Government

CREATIVE PARTNERS

Ainslie and Gorman Arts Centres

CANBERRA **THEATRE** CENTRE

PROGRAM PARTNERS

HOLDING REDLICH

ActewAGL

PRODUCTION SPONSORS

Sidestage

ELECT PRINTING

PRODUCERS CIRCLE

MAJOR DONORS

THE
JEREMY SPENCER BROOM
LEGACY

PRODUCERS CIRCLE

MICHAEL ADENA & JOANNE DALY
AMY CRAWFORD
PAUL & SHOBNA GOODING
MELINDA HILLERY

PETER & CASSANDRA HOOLIHAN
PETER & JANELLE MACGINLEY
TRACY NOBLE
RIDEAUX & FANNING FAMILY

CHRIS & ZOE WAGNER
ANONYMOUS (3)
as of June 2023

If you would like to know more about how you can support us, or are interested in partnering with us, contact **luke@canberrayouththeatre.com.au**

CANBERRA YOUTH THEATRE

STAFF

ARTISTIC DIRECTOR & CEO
LUKE ROGERS

ADMINISTRATOR
HELEN WOJTAS

ASSOCIATE PRODUCER
BONNIE CURTIS

FINANCE & STRATEGY MANAGER
LOUISE DAVIDSON

MARKETING & ENGAGEMENT MANAGER
CHRISTOPHER CARROLL

WORKSHOPS MANAGER
BETH AVERY

MARKETING & WORKSHOPS COORDINATOR
LACHLAN HOUEN

RESIDENT ARTISTS

EMILY AUSTIN   PATRICK HAESLER
ETHAN HAMILL   AISLINN KING
RHILEY WINNETT

COMMISSIONED WRITERS

HONOR WEBSTER-MANNISON

BOARD

PETER HOOLIHAN (CHAIR)
ADRIANA LAW (DEPUTY CHAIR)
CASSANDRA HOOLIHAN (SECRETARY)
ELLEN HARVEY (TREASURER)
AMY CRAWFORD
JOANNA ERSKINE
CELIA RIDEAUX
MEL ZIARNO

WORKSHOP ARTISTS

CAITLIN BAKER
ELLA BUCKLEY
ASHLEIGH BUTLER
CHRISTOPHER CARROLL
ELLIOT CLEAVES
REBECCA DUKE
QUINN GOODWIN
TOBI ODUSOTE
RACHEL ROBERTSON
LILY WELLING

GORMAN ARTS CENTRE
BATMAN STREET BRADDON ACT 2612
02 6248 5057
INFO@CANBERRAYOUTHTHEATRE.COM.AU

CANBERRAYOUTHTHEATRE.COM.AU

@canberrayouththeatre

www.ingramcontent.com/pod-product-compliance
Lightning Source LLC
Chambersburg PA
CBHW050017090426
42734CB00021B/3304